PAGE 109 C

MW01153300

Southern Living® Cookbook Library

The Seafood Cookbook

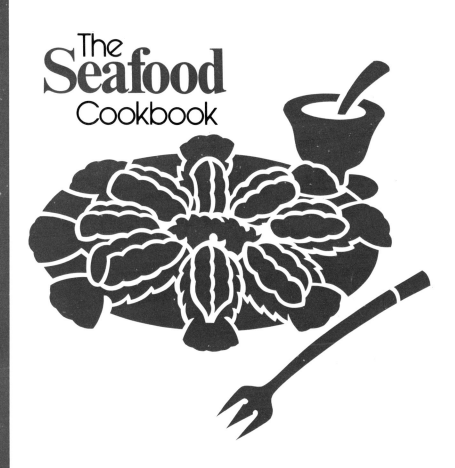

Cover: Shrimp Tarragon with Pimento Rice (page 126)
Left: Bass Ferezana (page 76)

contents

Spicy Rock Lobster Boil (page 128)

preface

No area is more graciously endowed with an abundance of fresh seafood products than the South. From the icy inland brooks, lakes, and streams come every imaginable variety of freshwater fish. And from the uppermost reaches of the Southland, the Chesapeake Bay area, come the little neck clams and hard- and soft-shell crabs as well as many saltwater fish. The warm waters of the Atlantic and Gulf of Mexico abound with many delicious saltwater fish and an excellent supply of spiny lobsters, shrimp, and crabs.

With such a tremendous variety of fish and shellfish to choose from, it is no wonder that a seafood cookbook was created. And a unique cookbook it is, too! This Southern Living *Seafood Cookbook* contains hundreds of seafood recipes, many of which are native southern favorites. As added features, color photographs accompanied by brief descriptions of the most common seafood cooking methods as well as convenient availability, cooking, and seasoning charts have all been included.

Yes, this *Seafood Cookbook* is an unusual cookbook that treats the many facets of seafood cookery expertly and thoroughly. It contains a diverse and lasting collection of genuine southern recipes that you will enjoy preparing again and again. So, from our kitchens to yours, welcome to the wonderful world of seafood cooking — southern style.

4

Most seafood can be cooked by any of the following methods: broiling, grilling, deep-frying, poaching, steaming, baking, panfrying, and sauteeing. On the basis of their natural fat content, fish are classified as either lean or fatty.

Lean fish such as haddock, cod, flounder and perch are especially suited to poaching or steaming. Their flesh is firm and does not easily flake during cooking. With proper preparation, they can also be successfully cooked by one of the dry heat methods, but, unlike fatty fish, require frequent basting with fat or oil.

Fatty fish such as shad, salmon, and mackerel need no special attention during broiling or grilling.

HOW TO
cook seafood

Shellfish, like lean fish, are also liberally basted during broiling, grilling, or baking to preserve the juicy texture. The major precaution in all seafood cookery is *never* to overcook the fish or shellfish.

TO MARINATE

The marinade you choose should complement the delicate flavor of your seafood. Pour the marinade over fish or shellfish. Marinate for several hours, then broil, charcoal grill, or bake, using the marinade as a basting sauce.

TO CHARCOAL GRILL

Fish and shellfish will cook quickly on an outdoor grill. Place the seafood on a well greased wire grill about 4 inches from moderately hot coals. To insure juiciness in the fish generously baste the seafood while it cooks with a sauce that contains some fat.

TO BROIL

Place your seafood on a well greased rack about 3 to 4 inches from the heat source. Brush the seafood liberally with melted butter, fat, or oil. Turn thick steaks and whole fish once, basting again before broiling on the other side. Fillets, split fish, and most shellfish need not be turned.

TO DEEP-FRY

Deep-frying is the quickest way to cook seafood. Fill a heavy 3- to 4-quart saucepan half-full with vegetable oil and heat slowly to 350 degrees. A thermometer will help you check the temperature accurately. Dip the sea-

food into milk, then coat with flour or coating mixture. Place one layer of breaded seafood in a fryer basket and lower into the hot oil. Fry until the seafood is golden brown; drain and serve immediately.

TO STEAM

Steaming entails cooking the fish or shellfish over a seasoned liquid depending upon specific recipes. In a Dutch oven, deep electric skillet, or baking dish, bring the liquid to a boil. Place the seafood on a greased perforated rack in the pan — above the level of the liquid. Cover the pan tightly and cook over the boiling water until the seafood is done. Season and salt the seafood after steaming.

TO BAKE

Baking is another popular dry heat method of cooking seafood. It differs from broiling and charcoal grilling in that the cooking temperature is lower and there is usually moisture present in the baking pan for basting. Lean and fatty fish alike including whole fish, steaks, fillets, and stuffed fish are suited to baking as are most types of shellfish. A moderately hot preheated oven of 400 to 425 degrees is recommended for baking. This temperature allows the seafood to cook quickly with only a minimum loss of natural moisture. At a lower temperature, the flesh is apt to dry out during the prolonged cooking period.

Line the bottom of a shallow baking pan with aluminum foil and grease the foil. Lay the fish or shellfish in the prepared pan.

Lard lean fish with bacon strips. Brush both lean and fatty fish generously with fat or oil.

Place the pan containing the fish in a preheated oven. You should allow 8 to 10 minutes cooking time per pound. But the actual cooking time will depend on the thickness of the cut. See the chart on page 188 or follow your recipe for suggested baking times of the various cuts of fish.

TO POACH

Poaching or simmering produces fine fish dishes. A poaching liquid may be a fish stock, court bouillon, or wine mixture. Place the fish on the flat, greased tray of a poacher or, if one is not available, on a strip of heavy-duty foil or cheesecloth. Lower this caddy into a pan and cover the fish with a boiling

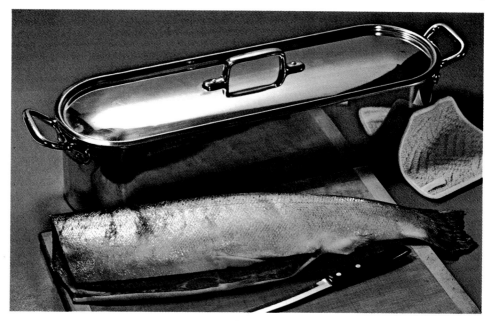

seasoned liquid. Cover the poacher and simmer gently just until the fish is cooked and flakes easily. Then remove it from the liquid; this liquid is often used to prepare a complementary sauce. The cooking time is determined by the size and thickness of the fish being poached.

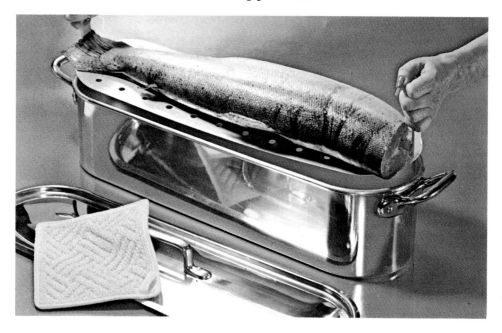

TO SAUTE AND PANFRY

These two similar methods of cooking fish and shellfish are probably the most widely used. Each involves cooking the seafood in a skillet containing only a small amount of fat. For sauteeing butter is used; for panfrying, vegetable oil is best. Unlike deep-frying, the seafood is never completely covered by the fat. Small whole fish, steaks and fillets, as well as soft-shelled crabs and oysters are well suited to either of these cooking methods.

Sauteeing — Dip cleaned seafood in milk and lightly dust with flour. Melt enough butter in a skillet to cover the bottom about 1/8-inch thick. When the butter is hot, but not burned, place the seafood in the skillet. Cook until gently browned on each side, turning once.

Panfrying — Mix together 1 egg and 1 tablespoon milk. Dip cleaned seafood in this mixture, then dredge in flour, cornmeal, cracker or bread crumbs. Heat enough cooking oil in a skillet to cover the bottom about 1/8-inch thick. When the oil is almost smoking, add the seafood to the hot oil and brown on each side, turning once.

TESTING FOR DONENESS

Test your fish or shellfish for doneness near the end of the suggested cooking time. Consult the seafood cooking chart on page 188 to help you determine the correct time for a particular cut. Pierce the seafood with a fork; when the flesh flakes easily, the fish is done. If the flesh is still somewhat elastic, more cooking time is required.

The following charts have been designed for your convenience. The *Seafood Availability Chart* shows seasonal fluctuations in the supply of fish and shellfish in the South as well as the most common market forms and the recommended cooking methods. Some regional variation in the fresh supply may occur. But many of the varieties listed are often available canned or frozen on a year-round basis.

You will notice that separate charts for fresh- and salt-water fish and shellfish have been designed. They will assist you in finding at a glance the information you need. For more detailed information on the recommended cooking methods, consult the section on *How to Cook Seafood* on page 6, or the *Fish Cooking Guide* on page 188.

SEAFOOD
availability chart

Saltwater Fish	Season	Market Form	Recommended Cooking Method
Bass	Year-round	Fresh: Whole, Steaks, Fillets; Frozen Fillets	Fry, saute, bake, broil, poach
Cod	Year-round, especially from September to December	Fresh: Whole, Steaks, Fillets; Frozen: Steaks, Fillets; Salted; Canned	Fry, saute, bake broil, grill, poach, steam
Flounder	Year-round	Fresh and Frozen Whole, Fillets	Fry, saute, bake, broil, grill
Haddock	Year-round	Fresh: Whole, Fillets, Steaks; Frozen Fillets; Smoked (as finnan haddie); Canned	Fry, saute, bake, broil, poach, steam, chowder
Halibut	Year-round	Fresh: Whole (by the pound), Steak, Fillets; Smoked Fillets	Fry, saute, bake, broil, grill, poach, steam
Mackerel	Spring to fall	Fresh: Whole, Steaks, Fillets; Frozen Fillets; Pickled; Salted; Smoked	Fry, saute, bake, broil, grill, poach, steam
Mullet	Year-round	Fresh: Whole, Fillets; Smoked	Fry, saute, bake, broil, grill, poach
Ocean Perch	Year-round	Frozen: Fillets, Steaks	Fry, saute, bake, broil, poach
Pompano	Year-round	Fresh: Whole, Fillets	Saute, bake, broil, poach
Red Snapper	Year-round especially summer and winter	Fresh: Whole, Fillets, Steaks	Fry, saute, bake, broil, poach
Salmon	Year-round, especially summer and fall	Fresh and Frozen: Steaks, Fillets; Smoked; Kippered; Salted; Canned	Fry, saute, bake, broil, poach, steam

Saltwater Fish	Season	Market Form	Recommended Cooking Method
Shad	January to July	Fresh and Frozen Boned; Fresh and Canned Roes	Fry, saute, bake, broil, grill
Sole	Year-round	Fresh: Whole, Fillets; Genuine Dover Sole only frozen	Fry, saute, bake, broil, grill, poach
Swordfish	June to October	Fresh and Frozen: Steaks, Fillets	Bake, broil, grill, steam
Tuna	Year-round	Fresh: Whole, Fillets Steaks; Smoked; Canned	Bake, broil, grill, steam
Whiting	Year-round, especially summer and fall	Fresh and Frozen: Whole, Fillets; Smoked	Saute, bake, broil, poach

Freshwater Fish	Season	Market Form	Recommended Cooking Method
Bass	Year-round	Fresh whole	Fry, saute, bake, broil
Brook Trout	Year-round	Fresh and Frozen: Whole, Fillets; Smoked	Fry, bake, broil, poach
Catfish	Year-round	Fresh: Whole, Fillets	Fry, saute, bake, broil, poach
Perch	Year-round	Fresh: Whole, Fillets; Frozen fillets	Fry, saute, bake, broil
Pike	Year-round	Fresh: Whole, Fillets; Frozen whole	Fry, bake, broil, poach
Whitefish	April to December	Fresh: Whole, Fillets; Smoked	Saute, bake, broil, poach, steam

Shellfish	Season	Market Form	Recommended Cooking Method
Clams-hard and soft	Year-round	Fresh; Canned; Shucked; Pickled	Raw, steam, fry, chowder
Crab-hard soft	Year-round May to September	Fresh; Cooked in shell; Canned; Iced; Smoked	Boil, steam, saute
King	Year-round	Frozen legs; Canned	Broil, bake
Lobster Northern	Year-round	Fresh, Canned, and Cooked in shell; Lobster Meat;	Broil, boil
Rock	Year-round	Frozen tails in shell	Broil
Mussels	Spring and summer	Fresh; Canned; Pickled; Smoked	Raw, boil, steam, broil
Oysters	September to April	Fresh in shell; Shelled in liquid; Frozen; Smoked	Raw, steam, fry, bake
Scallops Sea Bay	Year-round, especially spring, fall, winter	Fresh; Frozen; Canned Fresh; Frozen; Canned	Fry, saute, broil, bake
Shrimp	Year-round, especially spring and summer	Fresh in shell, Shelled; Frozen in shell, Shelled; Canned	Boil, fry, saute, broil, bake

Festive Seafood Cocktail Sauce (page 30)

seafood appetizers

There are few foods more appealing than an assortment of appetizers. And seafood is the logical choice because its mild flavor is extremely compatible with many highly or unusually seasoned foods. In fact, the variety of foods with which fish and shellfish can be combined is genuinely impressive. And yet no matter how unconventional an appetizer you concoct, seafood is still light enough to simply whet the appetite and not dull it.

In the following chapter you will find a diverse collection of seafood appetizers. Many of these recipes, like Clams Casino, have been selected for their expert use of seasonings. You will certainly enjoy this elegant appetizer prepared from clams, anchovy paste, lemon, onion, green pepper, pimento, and bacon.

Also included in this chapter are many appetite-arousing recipes for finger foods such as Savory Bites — which incidentally truly lives up to its name. Marinate shrimp in French dressing seasoned with capers, celery seed, and Tabasco sauce for several hours. You will be pleasantly surprised at the distinctive taste of the shrimp. Another such delicious finger food is Smoked Oyster Roll-Ups. Slices of crisp bacon are rolled around smoked oysters, fastened with toothpicks, and warmed in an oven.

Turn to this chapter often for an unusual and diverse selection of seafood appetizers.

Omelette Parcels (below)

OMELETTE PARCELS

1 c. minced fillet of pork	1/2 tsp. sugar
10 deveined shrimp, chopped	1/4 tsp. freshly grated ginger
2 tbsp. minced leek	1 tsp. cornstarch
1 clove of garlic, minced	4 eggs
1 tbsp. soy sauce	1 1/2 tbsp. margarine

Combine all the ingredients except the eggs and the margarine and mix well. Beat the eggs with a fork. Melt a small amount of the margarine in a small omelet pan, then pour in enough of the egg to cover bottom of pan. Fry on one side, then place 1 teaspoon of the pork mixture in center of unfried side. Fold the edges over to form a pocket and press together. Place on rack over water in steamer pan, then fry the remaining eggs until all the margarine, eggs and filling are used. Cover and steam for 10 to 15 minutes. Remove from steamer and serve immediately with Chinese soy sauce or a strong Chinese chili sauce.

APPETIZER DELUXE

1 can sm. shrimp	Juice of 3 lemons
1 can crab	Dash of garlic salt
1 can grapefruit sections	Dash of onion salt
1 bottle catsup	Dash of salt
1 No. 2 1/2 can tomato juice	Dash of Worcestershire sauce

Drain the shrimp, crab and grapefruit sections, then cut the shrimp and grapefruit into small pieces. Mix the catsup, tomato juice, lemon juice and seasonings together and pour over the shrimp mixture. Mix well and refrigerate for several hours before serving. 12 servings.

Mrs. Pat Fisher, Houston, Texas

SEAFOOD COCKTAIL

1 pkg. frozen shrimp	1 c. chili sauce
2 pkg. frozen lobster	1 c. mayonnaise
1 can crab meat	Salt and pepper to taste
1 tbsp. prepared mustard	1 sm. onion, grated
1 tsp. dry mustard	Horseradish to taste
1 tsp. Worcestershire sauce	

Cook the shrimp and lobster according to package directions. Cool and cut into small pieces. Combine the shrimp, lobster and crab meat and chill thoroughly. Combine the remaining ingredients and pour over the seafood. Toss to mix well. Serve in cocktail glasses. 12 servings.

Mrs. Alan Kadet, Southside, Florida

ANCHOVY ROLL-UPS

1 3-oz. package cream cheese	1 tsp. Worcestershire sauce
1 tbsp. milk	6 to 8 slices bread
2 tsp. anchovy paste	3 tbsp. melted butter

Soften the cream cheese and blend with the milk until creamy. Blend in the anchovy paste and Worcestershire sauce. Trim the crust from the bread and spread with anchovy mixture. Cut in half, then roll up and wrap in waxed paper. Chill thoroughly. Melt the butter in a skillet and saute the rolls. Serve hot on toothpicks.

Mrs. Ben W. Fisher, Dallas, Texas

CAVIAR FORTE

1 4-oz. jar caviar	3 tbsp. mayonnaise
1 med. onion, minced	Juice of 1 lemon

Combine all the ingredients in a small bowl, then chill thoroughly. Serve with crackers.

Helen Iffla Bay, Clearwater, Florida

17

CLAMS CASINO

36 cherrystone clams	1/4 c. minced onion
3/4 c. cornmeal	1/4 c. minced green pepper
Rock salt	2 tbsp. diced pimento
1/4 c. butter	Salt and pepper to taste
1 tsp. anchovy paste	4 strips bacon, diced
Juice of 1/2 lemon	

Place the clams in a large pan and cover with cold salted water. Sprinkle cornmeal over water. Let stand for about 4 hours. Scrub the shells, then open and drain the clams. Arrange 36 half shells on bed of rock salt in large, shallow baking tray. Mix the butter and anchovy paste together and place 1/4 teaspoon in each half shell. Sprinkle the lemon juice on the clams and place in the shells. Combine the onion, green pepper and pimento and spread over the clams. Sprinkle with salt and pepper. Top with bacon. Bake at 450 degrees for 15 minutes or until bacon is browned. 8-10 servings.

Mrs. Donald Bertolet, Quincey, Florida

SPICY CLAM APPETIZER

2 cans flaky refrigerator baking powder biscuits	1/4 c. chili sauce
1 10 1/2-oz. can minced clams, drained	1/4 c. sour cream
	Grated American cheese

Preheat the oven to 400 degrees. Separate each biscuit into 2 layers and place on ungreased cookie sheets. Combine the clams, chili sauce and sour cream. Spread about 1 tablespoon of the clam mixture on each biscuit half, then sprinkle with cheese. Bake for 10 to 12 minutes or until golden brown. Serve warm.

Mrs. James J. Zapalac, Austin County, Texas

CHERRY-O-CRAB DELIGHTS

40 cherry tomatoes	1/2 tsp. salt
1 6 1/2-oz. can crab meat	1/2 tsp. celery seed
1 3-oz. package cream cheese, softened	1/4 tsp. seasoned pepper
2 tbsp. sour cream	1/4 tsp. seasoned salt
2 tsp. white wine	1/8 tsp. onion salt
1 tbsp. minced parsley	1/8 tsp. paprika

Remove the stems from the tomatoes and cut off enough top to make small caps. Scoop out the pulp. Drain the crab meat thoroughly and flake. Combine the remaining ingredients and blend in crab meat. Fill the tomatoes with the crab meat mixture. Stick a toothpick through the center of the cap and gently stick into the stuffed tomato to hold together. Garnish with sprig of fresh parsley.

Mrs. Jean Brown, Danville, Kentucky

Crab Dabs (below)

CRAB DABS

1 12-oz. can dungeness crab meat	1 tsp. chopped chives
1/3 c. fine soft bread crumbs	1 tsp. dry mustard
2 tbsp. dry sherry	1/4 tsp. salt
	10 slices bacon, cut in thirds

Drain the crab meat, then remove any remaining shell or cartilage. Chop the crab meat. Combine all the ingredients except the bacon and mix thoroughly. Chill for 30 minutes. Portion the crab mixture with a tablespoon, then shape into small rolls. Wrap bacon around crab rolls and secure with a toothpick. Place crab rolls on a broiler pan. Broil about 4 inches from source of heat for 8 to 10 minutes or until bacon is crisp. Turn carefully. Broil for 4 to 5 minutes longer or until bacon is crisp. 30 hors d'oeuvres.

CRAB-BACON ROLLS

1/2 c. tomato juice	1 tsp. chopped parsley
1 egg, well beaten	1 tsp. chopped celery leaves
1 c. dry bread crumbs	1 6 1/2-oz. can crab meat,
Dash of salt	drained
Dash of pepper	12 slices bacon, halved

Mix the tomato juice and egg, then add the crumbs, seasonings, parsley, celery leaves and crab meat. Mix thoroughly and roll into finger lengths. Wrap each roll with 1/2 slice bacon and fasten with a toothpick. Place on rack in broiler pan. Broil, turning frequently, until brown.

Mrs. Frank White Houston, Grenada, Mississippi

CRAB-CHEESE FONDUE

1 lb. butter	1 can crab meat, drained
1 lb. Cheddar cheese, cubed	1 loaf French bread

Place the butter and cheese in a fondue pot and cook over medium heat, stirring constantly, until ingredients are melted and mixed. Add the crab meat and heat through. Place over low flame. Cut the bread in cubes. Spear the bread cubes with fondue forks and dip into crab mixture.

Mrs. Earl Campbell, Montgomery, Alabama

CRAB FLIP

1 7 1/2-oz. can crab meat	1/4 c. finely chopped celery
1 hard-boiled egg, chopped	Mayonnaise

Drain the crab meat and mix with the egg and celery. Add enough mayonnaise to moisten. Serve with crackers.

Irene Loveless, Pecos, Texas

CRAB MEAT CANAPES

4 green peppers	1 tsp. grated onion
1 c. flaked crab meat	2 tbsp. minced parsley
2 tbsp. olive or corn oil	1/2 tsp. lemon juice

Cut the green peppers into 1 1/2-inch squares. Then combine the remaining ingredients in a blender container and blend until smooth. Spread the crab mixture on the green pepper squares and serve on cocktail picks.

Mrs. Roy Walters, Cape Coral, Florida

GRAPEFRUIT AND CRAB MEAT COCKTAIL

1 No. 2 can grapefruit sections	1 tbsp. vinegar
1 6 1/2-oz. can crab meat	1 tsp. lemon juice
1 c. mayonnaise	2 tbsp. catsup
	1 drop of hot sauce

Drain and chill the grapefruit sections. Drain and flake the crab meat, then chill thoroughly. Alternate the grapefruit and crab meat in 8 cocktail glasses. Mix the remaining ingredients and pour over the top.

Mrs. Gladys Willar, Pompano Beach, Florida

PUFFY CRAB CANAPES

2 egg whites	Salt and pepper to taste
1 c. mayonnaise	Bread slices
1 c. flaked crab meat	

Beat the egg whites until stiff peaks form, then fold in the mayonnaise, crab meat and seasonings. Cut the bread into desired shapes and toast on one side. Spread the untoasted side with the crab mixture. Broil until heated through and lightly browned.

Mrs. C. R. Butler, Summit, Mississippi

GOURMET CRAB CANAPES

1 can refrigerator crescent dinner rolls	1/4 tsp. Worcestershire sauce
1 6 1/2-oz. can crab meat	1/3 c. sour cream
1/4 c. chili sauce	

Separate the rolls and cut each triangle into 4 small triangles. Drain and flake the crab meat, then combine with the chili sauce and Worcestershire sauce. Spread 1 teaspoon of the crab mixture on each triangle. Place on an ungreased cookie sheet and top with 1/2 teaspoon sour cream. Bake at 375 degrees for 10 minutes or until golden brown. Serve warm.

Mrs. Clifford Seales, Mobile, Alabama

HOT CRAB MEAT SPREAD

1 8-oz. package cream cheese	1 can crab meat, drained
3 tbsp. milk	Paprika
1 tsp. minced onion	Slivered almonds
1 tsp. cream-style horseradish	Party rye bread slices

Soften the cream cheese, then blend with the milk until creamy. Add the onion, horseradish and crab meat and mix until well blended. Place in a small baking dish and sprinkle with paprika and almonds. Bake at 350 degrees for 10 minutes or until heated through. Serve as spread for rye bread.

Mrs. Ben W. Fisher, Dallas, Texas

OLIVE-CRAB DEVILED EGGS

6 hard-cooked eggs	1/3 c. chopped celery
1 6 1/2-oz. can crab meat	1/4 c. mayonnaise
1/4 c. chopped Spanish green olives	1/4 tsp. dry mustard

Cut the eggs in half lengthwise and remove the yolks. Mash the yolks. Drain the crab meat and mix into the egg yolks. Add the olives, celery, mayonnaise and mustard and mix well. Fill the egg whites with the yolk mixture, then chill thoroughly before serving.

Mrs. Marvin Boone, Bay Minette, Alabama

LOBSTER FLORIDIAN

1 8-oz. package cream cheese	1 tsp. prepared mustard
1/4 c. mayonnaise or salad dressing	1 tsp. grated onion
1 clove of garlic, crushed	Dash of seasoned salt
1 tsp. sugar	1 5-oz. can lobster
	3 tbsp. sauterne

Melt the cream cheese in blazer pan of small chafing dish over low heat, stirring constantly. Blend in the mayonnaise, garlic, sugar, mustard, onion and seasoned salt. Drain and flake the lobster, then remove cartilage. Add to cream cheese mixture. Add the sauterne and heat through, stirring frequently. Keep warm over hot water. Serve with melba toast and assorted crackers. About 1 3/4 cups.

Mrs. Frank Whitehead, Tucson, Arizona

AVOCADO-LOBSTER COCKTAIL

2 med. ripe avocados	1/4 c. tarragon vinegar
1 1/2 lb.-can lobster	1 tsp. onion juice
1/2 c. sharp French dressing	2 tsp. chopped parsley
1 c. mayonnaise	

Cut the avocado in half and remove the seed, then peel. Cut into small chunks and place in bowl. Cut the lobster into bite-sized pieces and add to the avocado. Pour the dressing over the lobster and toss lightly to combine. Cover and chill for at least 2 hours. Turn into sherbet glasses. Combine the remaining ingredients and spoon over the lobster mixture. Serve immediately. 6 servings.

Mrs. Jane Crockett, Bristol, Tennessee

LOBSTER COCKTAIL

4 tbsp. chili sauce	1 tsp. Worcestershire sauce
2 tbsp. lemon juice	3/4 tsp. salt
8 drops of hot sauce	1 sm. can lobster
3 tbsp. minced celery	

Combine the first 6 ingredients and mix well. Cut the lobster into small pieces and add to the sauce. Chill thoroughly. Serve in cocktail glasses.

Mrs. B. L. Harrington, Raleigh, North Carolina

SMOKED OYSTER ROLL-UPS

1 lb. bacon	1 can smoked oysters

Cut the bacon strips in half. Fry the bacon until almost done, but not crisp. Drain and cool. Drain the oysters on paper towel, then wrap bacon around oysters. Fasten with toothpick. Bake at 375 degrees until bacon is crisp.

Mrs. Ann Kelly, Charleston, South Carolina

Oyster Cocktail with Sauce (below)

OYSTER COCKTAIL WITH SAUCE

2 tbsp. prepared horseradish
3/4 c. tomato catsup
3 tbsp. chili sauce
2 tbsp. lemon juice

Salt to taste
Dash of hot sauce
Oysters on the half shell

Combine all the ingredients except the oysters and mix well. Place in a small bowl in the center of tray. Surround with oysters.

OYSTERS ROCKEFELLER

5 tbsp. butter
1/2 c. drained chopped
    spinach
2 tbsp. minced onion
2 tsp. minced celery
3 tbsp. fine dry crumbs

1/4 tsp. herb blend for fish
1/4 tsp. anchovy paste
1/4 tsp. salt
Pinch of pepper
24 oysters in shells

Melt the butter in a saucepan, then add the spinach, onion, celery, crumbs, herb blend, anchovy paste, salt and pepper. Mix well and heat through. Remove the oysters from the shells and set aside. Scrub the shells and place in bed of hot rock salt in baking pan. Place oyster in each shell. Broil slowly for 5 minutes. Place 1 teaspoon of the spinach mixture on each oyster. Broil until heated through. Serve immediately. 4 servings.

Mrs. Victor A. Maola, Wichita Falls, Texas

OYSTERS BIENVILLE

Ice cream salt	1 egg yolk
1 bunch green onions and	1/3 c. white wine
tops	1 tsp. salt
2 tbsp. butter	Dash of cayenne pepper
2 tbsp. flour	2 doz. oysters, in shells
2/3 c. chicken broth	1/2 c. French bread crumbs
1/3 c. mushroom pieces	1 tbsp. Parmesan cheese

Preheat oven to 400 degrees. Pour a layer of ice cream salt in a shallow pan, then set pan in oven to heat through. Mince the onions, then saute in butter in a skillet over low heat for about 6 minutes or until tender. Add the flour and cook, stirring, until brown. Stir in the chicken broth and mushrooms. Beat the egg yolk with the wine, then add to the sauce slowly, beating rapidly. Season with salt and cayenne pepper. Cook for 10 to 15 minutes over low heat, stirring constantly. Drain the oysters and place 1 on each half shell. Press the shells into the hot salt in pan. Bake for 5 minutes. Spoon sauce over each oyster. Combine the bread crumbs and cheese and sprinkle over the sauce. Return to oven and bake for about 15 minutes longer or until lightly browned. 4 servings.

Mrs. Ann Gernhauser, Chalmette, Louisiana

NOR'EAST NIBBLES

16 frozen fried fish sticks	2 tbsp. butter or margarine
1/2 c. grated Parmesan cheese	Sea Sauce

Cut the frozen fish sticks into thirds, then roll each piece in the cheese. Melt the butter in a 15 x 10 x 1-inch baking pan. Place the fish in the pan. Bake at 450

Nor'east Nibbles (above)

degrees for 8 to 10 minutes. Turn carefully. Bake for 8 to 10 minutes longer or until crisp and brown. Drain on absorbent paper. Serve with hot Sea Sauce.

Sea Sauce

1 8-oz. can tomato sauce	1/4 tsp. hot sauce
1/4 c. chili sauce	1/4 tsp. thyme
1/4 tsp. garlic powder	1/8 tsp. sugar
1/4 tsp. oregano	Dash of basil

Combine all the ingredients in a small saucepan and simmer for 10 to 12 minutes, stirring occasionally.

COQUILLES SAINT JACQUES

Lemon juice	Dash of pepper
1/2 tsp. salt	1 c. light cream
2 lb. sea scallops, drained	1/2 c. milk
6 tbsp. butter or margarine	1 c. grated Gruyere cheese
1/4 c. finely chopped onion	1/2 c. dry white wine
1/4 lb. mushrooms, sliced	1 tbsp. chopped parsley
1/3 c. flour	1/2 c. dry bread crumbs

Combine 1 cup water, 1 teaspoon lemon juice and salt in a saucepan and bring to a boil. Add the scallops and simmer, covered, for 6 minutes or until tender. Drain on paper towels. Melt 4 tablespoons butter in a medium saucepan, then add the onion and mushrooms and saute for about 5 minutes or until tender. Remove from heat and stir in flour and pepper until well blended. Stir in the cream and milk gradually, then bring to a boil, stirring constantly. Reduce heat and simmer, stirring frequently, for 4 to 5 minutes or until thick. Add the cheese and stir until melted. Remove from heat. Stir in wine, 1 tablespoon lemon juice and parsley, then add the scallops. Turn into small scallop shells. Mix the bread crumbs and remaining melted butter and sprinkle over the scallops. Place the shells on a cookie sheet. Broil 4 inches from heat for 2 to 3 minutes or until golden brown.

Mrs. Oliver B. Pinkney, Covington, Virginia

SALMON FONDUE

1 8-oz. can salmon	1 c. milk
2 tbsp. butter	1 1/2 c. grated Swiss cheese
3 tbsp. flour	

Drain the salmon and reserve liquid. Add enough water to reserved liquid to make 1/2 cup liquid. Melt the butter in top of double boiler and stir in the flour. Add the salmon liquid and stir until smooth. Add the milk and cook over simmering water until thickened. Add the cheese and cook, stirring, until cheese melts. Remove bones from salmon and flake salmon. Add to cheese sauce and heat through. Place in a fondue pot and keep warm over low flame.

Mrs. Fred Cook, Cove, Arkansas

Smoky Salmon (below)

SMOKY SALMON

1 7 3/4-oz. can salmon	1 tsp. grated onion
1/4 c. mayonnaise	1/4 tsp. liquid smoke
1 tbsp. lemon juice	Pastry for 1-crust pie
1 tsp. horseradish	Paprika

Drain and flake the salmon. Add the mayonnaise and seasonings and mix thoroughly. Divide the pastry in half, then roll out each half into a thin 9-inch circle. Spread each circle with 1/2 cup of the salmon mixture. Cut into 16 wedge-shaped pieces and roll in jelly roll fashion, beginning at the round edge. Place the rolls on a baking sheet, then prick top. Sprinkle with paprika. Bake at 450 degrees for 10 to 15 minutes or until lightly browned. 32 hors d'oeuvres.

MARINATED SHRIMP

2 lb. frozen shelled shrimp	12 capers
1 egg	1 tbsp. caper juice
1 1/4 c. salad oil	1 tbsp. Worcestershire sauce
Juice of 2 lemons	1 c. chili sauce
1/2-in. square lemon peel	1 tsp. salt
1 sm. onion	

Cook the shrimp according to package directions and remove veins. Place in a bowl. Place the egg in a blender. Add remaining ingredients, one at a time, blending well after each addition. Pour over the shrimp and refrigerate overnight. Drain the shrimp and place on a tray. Garnish as desired. 8-12 servings.

Mrs. S. S. Koru, Gainesville, Florida

BUTTERY SHRIMP

6 lb. fresh shrimp	2 cloves of garlic, minced
3/4 c. butter or margarine	1 1/2 tsp. salt
3/4 c. chopped parsley	

Shell and devein the shrimp. Melt the butter in a large frying pan, then add the parsley, garlic and salt. Heat, stirring, until bubbly. Add the shrimp and saute, stirring frequently, for about 8 minutes or until shrimp turn pink. Keep warm. Place in chafing dish as needed and garnish with lemon slices. 25 servings.

Mrs. John Collins, Mesa, Arizona

CHARCOAL-BROILED SHRIMP

24 fresh jumbo shrimp	12 slices bacon, halved
24 anchovy fillets	

Shell the shrimp, then split down the back, removing the sand vein. Insert an anchovy in each slit. Wrap in bacon and secure with a pick. Broil over charcoal until bacon is crisp. 6 servings.

Mrs. Helen Taylor, Newport, Kentucky

CREAMY SHRIMP DIP

1 8-oz. package cream cheese	1/2 tsp. Worcestershire sauce
	2 tsp. lemon juice
2 c. boiled shrimp, minced	Salt to taste
1 c. sour cream	4 to 6 drops of hot sauce

Combine all the ingredients, blending well. Chill for 2 to 3 hours. Serve with potato chips and crackers.

Nancy J. Lea, Jacksonville, Florida

SCAMPI WITH CAPER SAUCE

1/2 c. olive oil	2 lb. shrimp, deveined
2 cloves of garlic, minced	1/2 c. mayonnaise
2 tbsp. Worcestershire sauce	1 tbsp. lemon juice
1/4 c. minced parsley	2 tbsp. drained capers
1/2 tsp. crumbled oregano	1/2 tsp. monosodium glutamate

Heat the olive oil in a skillet, then add the garlic, Worcestershire sauce, parsley, oregano and shrimp. Cook, stirring constantly, until shrimp are golden brown. Combine the mayonnaise, lemon juice, capers and monosodium glutamate and mix well. Serve with the shrimp. 4 servings.

Mrs. Lenore Prescott, Yuma, Arizona

27

Italian Scampi (below)

ITALIAN SCAMPI

1 lb. medium shrimp	1 tbsp. chopped parsley
1/4 c. margarine	1/4 tsp. salt
1 clove of garlic, minced	Dash of pepper
1 1/2 tbsp. lemon juice	Dash of paprika

Shell, devein and drain the shrimp. Melt the margarine in a skillet over medium heat, then add the garlic and lemon juice. Simmer for 3 minutes, stirring frequently, then add the shrimp and saute for 4 to 5 minutes or until shrimp are pink and tender. Add the parsley, salt, pepper and paprika and mix. Turn into serving dish and serve on toothpicks.

SAVORY BITES

1 c. French dressing	4 to 5 drops of hot sauce
1 tbsp. capers and juice	1 lb. cooked shrimp
1/2 tsp. celery seed	

Combine the dressing and seasonings, then pour over the shrimp. Refrigerate overnight, then drain. Serve on salad greens on tray with cocktail picks.

Mrs. Terry Kuntz, Rudy, Arkansas

SHRIMP COCKTAIL

1/4 c. lemon juice	3/4 c. chili sauce
1/4 c. salad oil	1 tbsp. horseradish
1/4 tsp. seafood seasoning	2 tbsp. chopped onion
1/2 tsp. seasoned salt	2 lb. cleaned cooked shrimp

Combine all the ingredients except the shrimp in blender container. Process until well blended. Place the shrimp in a refrigerator container, then pour the sauce over shrimp. Cover and refrigerate for 24 hours, stirring occasionally. Serve in cocktail glasses.

Mrs. Della Goodson, Pensacola, Florida

SHRIMP-CHEESE FONDUE

1 can frozen cream of shrimp soup	**1 can shrimp, drained**
	3 tbsp. dry wine
1/2 lb. Swiss cheese, grated	**French bread, cubed**

Place the soup in a fondue pot. Add the cheese and heat until cheese is melted. Add the shrimp and wine. Place on a stand over low flame. Dip bread into cheese mixture to serve.

Mrs. R. L. Berry, Little Rock, Arkansas

SHRIMP ARNAUD

1/4 c. vinegar	**1/4 tsp. garlic salt**
1/4 c. salad oil	**1 tsp. prepared mustard**
1/4 c. chili sauce	**1 lb. shrimp, cooked**

Combine the vinegar, salad oil, chili sauce, garlic salt and mustard and mix well. Add the shrimp and toss to coat with sauce. Cover and refrigerate overnight. Serve with cocktail picks.

Mrs. Patti Green, New Orleans, Louisiana

SPICY SHRIMP

2 lb. shrimp	**1 1/4 c. salad oil**
1/2 c. celery tops	**3/4 c. white vinegar**
1/4 c. mixed pickling spices	**2 1/2 tbsp. capers and juice**
1 tbsp. salt	**2 1/2 tsp. celery seed**
2 med. onions, sliced	**Dash of hot sauce**
7 to 8 bay leaves	**Juice of 1 lemon**

Cover the shrimp with boiling water, then add the celery tops, pickling spices and salt. Cook for about 10 minutes, then drain. Cover with ice, then clean and devein. Alternate shrimp, onions and bay leaves in a shallow dish. Combine the remaining ingredients and pour over shrimp. Cover and refrigerate for at least 12 hours. Remove from dish with slotted spoon to serving dish.

Mrs. E. Kenneth Gavin, Tampa, Florida

CAVIAR MOUSSE

1 env. unflavored gelatin	**1/2 tsp. Worcestershire sauce**
2 oz. black caviar	**1/4 tsp. mustard**
3 sieved hard-boiled eggs	**1 tsp. minced onion**
2/3 c. mayonnaise	**Salt and pepper to taste**

Soften the gelatin in 1/4 cup cold water, then dissolve over hot water. Add the remaining ingredients. Pour into a wet mold and refrigerate for 5 to 6 hours. Unmold and serve with crackers.

Mrs. Deborah Peek, Birmingham, Alabama

FESTIVE SEAFOOD COCKTAIL SAUCE

1 1/2 c. catsup	1 1/2 tsp. sugar
1 tbsp. lemon juice	Dash of hot sauce
1 tbsp. Worcestershire sauce	Salt and pepper to taste

Combine all the ingredients and mix well. Chill thoroughly. Serve with fresh boiled shrimp or boiled lobster. Garnish with stuffed olives.

Photograph for this recipe on page 14.

SHRIMP DIP

1 8-oz. package cream cheese	1/2 tsp. Worcestershire sauce
3 tbsp. milk or cream	1 6-oz. can shrimp, drained
2 tbsp. grated onion	

Soften the cream cheese, then blend in the milk. Add the onion and Worcestershire sauce and beat until fluffy. Mash the shrimp, then blend into the cheese mixture. Serve with potato chips.

Judi Koehmstedt, Seminole, Florida

DELICIOUS SHRIMP FONDUE

1 split clove of garlic	Pepper and paprika to taste
2 cans frozen shrimp soup	Cooked peeled shrimp
1 c. milk	French bread, cut in
1 lb. Swiss cheese, grated	1-in. cubes

Rub a fondue pot with garlic. Place the soup in the fondue pot and heat, stirring, until smooth. Add the milk slowly and cook, stirring, until mixed. Add the cheese and stir until melted. Sprinkle with pepper and paprika and place over burner. Place the shrimp and bread on fondue forks and dip into cheese mixture.

Mrs. Dean Holmes, Warner Robbins, Georgia

SHRIMP-STUFFED EGGS

6 hard-cooked eggs, halved	1 tsp. minced onion
1 4 1/2-oz. can shrimp	1 tsp. Worcestershire sauce
1 tsp. salt	1 tbsp. lemon juice
1/2 c. mayonnaise	

Remove the yolks from the eggs and reserve the whites. Drain the shrimp and mash with the egg yolks. Add the remaining ingredients except the egg whites and mix well. Fill the egg whites with yolk mixture. Serve as appetizer.

Mrs. K. W. Rockett, Gloster, Mississippi

Maine Sardine Canapes (below)

MAINE SARDINE CANAPES

3 cans Maine sardines
1/2 c. butter, softened
2 tbsp. prepared mustard

10 slices sandwich bread
Pimento strips

Drain the sardines. Combine the butter and mustard and spread on the bread, then remove the crusts. Cut each slice of bread into thirds. Place a sardine on each piece of bread. Garnish with pimento strips.

CRISPY FRIED MAINE SARDINES

4 cans Maine sardines in
  tomato sauce
1 8-oz. can tomato sauce
1 c. dry bread crumbs

1/3 c. grated Parmesan cheese
1/2 c. flour
Cocktail sauce

Drain the sardines and reserve the sauce. Combine the tomato sauce and the reserved sardine sauce. Combine the crumbs and cheese. Roll the sardines in the flour, then dip in the tomato sauce and roll in the crumb mixture. Place in a single layer in a fry basket. Fry in deep 350-degree fat for 1 minute or until brown. Drain on absorbent paper. Serve with cocktail sauce.

FESTIVE SARDINE CANAPES

1 8-oz. package cream
  cheese, softened
6 drops of hot sauce
1/4 c. chili sauce
1 tbsp. lemon juice
1 tsp. olive juice

20 sm. stuffed olives,
  chopped
Dash of garlic salt
Oblong crackers
Sardines

Combine the cream cheese, hot sauce, chili sauce, lemon juice, olive juice, olives and garlic salt, then mix until well blended. Spread on crackers. Top each cracker with 1 sardine and garnish with olive slice.

Mrs. Laura Grenshaw, Lancaster, South Carolina

Apple-Tuna Mousse (page 50)

seafood salads

Seafood is prized as food throughout the South because there are so many varieties of marine fish and shellfish that abound in the coastal waters. For Southerners one of the most popular ways to serve seafood is in salads. Seafood salads are both easy to prepare and varied in taste. And there are so many interesting ingredients and dressings to complement the taste of fish and shellfish in salads.

One salad that you will find in the following section is Tossed Seafood Salad. This is a hot and hearty main dish salad that uses shrimp, lobster, and crabmeat. A delicate sour cream dressing completes its simple preparation. Another recipe entry that is surprisingly easy to fix is Lobster in Cucumber Shells. Fresh crisp cucumbers are fashioned into boats and generously filled with a mildly seasoned lobster salad. This dish is one of the easiest and most attractive salads you can prepare.

Also included in this chapter are specialty salads with a distinctively different flavor. One such interesting and exotic combination that you will want to try is Mandarin Shrimp Salad. Crunchy water chestnuts, mandarin oranges, whipped heavy cream, and shrimp are the main ingredients in this unusual dish. You will have to try it to believe it.

For ease of preparation and genuine flavor variety, turn to the seafood salads contained in this chapter.

BAKED NEPTUNE SALAD

1 green pepper, chopped	1/4 tsp. pepper
1 med. onion, chopped	1 tsp. Worcestershire sauce
1 c. chopped celery	1/2 c. mayonnaise
Butter	1/2 c. sour cream
1/2 lb. crab meat	1/4 c. sherry
1 c. cleaned shrimp	1 c. buttered crumbs
1 tsp. salt	

Saute the green pepper, onion and celery in a small amount of butter until limp. Add the remaining ingredients except the crumbs and mix well. Place in individual shells or greased casserole. Sprinkle with the crumbs. Bake at 350 degrees for 30 minutes. 8 servings.

Mrs. Lawrence Anderson, Ft. Eustis, Virginia

CURRIED SEAFOOD SALAD

1 7-oz. can solid-pack tuna	2 tbsp. lemon juice
1 c. cooked shrimp, cleaned	1 tsp. curry powder
1/2 c. celery, chopped	3 c. cold cooked rice
1/4 c. chopped ripe olives	3 tbsp. French dressing
1/2 c. mayonnaise	1/2 c. snipped parsley

Drain the tuna, then combine with the shrimp and chill thoroughly. Combine the celery, olives, mayonnnaise, lemon juice and curry powder, then blend in the tuna mixture. Toss the rice, French dressing and parsley together, then spoon onto serving platter. Top with the tuna mixture. 6 servings.

Mrs. Esther Sigmund, Laredo, Texas

SEA SALAD

2 lb. shrimp	2 avocados
1 tbsp. shrimp spice	Lemon juice
2 6-oz. packages frozen	Romaine lettuce leaves
King crab meat	1 lb. lump crab meat
1 10-oz. package frozen	1 c. mayonnaise
artichoke hearts	1/2 c. pineapple juice

Place the shrimp in a large saucepan, then cover with water and add the spice. Bring to a boil, then reduce heat and cook for about 10 minutes. Drain and rinse with cold water. Shell and devein. Thaw the King crab meat and drain. Cook the artichoke hearts according to package directions, then drain. Peel the avocados and remove the seeds, then slice. Dip the slices in lemon juice. Arrange the lettuce on platter, then place the shrimp, crab meat and King crab in rows on lettuce. Arrange the artichokes and avocados in rows between seafood. Chill thoroughly. Combine the mayonnaise and pineapple juice and serve with salad. 8 servings.

Mrs. Melvin H. Jones, Granite Falls, North Carolina

Seafood Caesar (below)

SEAFOOD CAESAR

6 c. torn salad greens	3/4 c. sliced boiled lobster-tails
3/4 c. croutons	1/2 c. crab meat
1 peeled avocado, diced	1 tomato
3/4 c. small cooked shrimp	3/4 c. Caesar dressing

Place the salad greens in a large salad bowl, then add the croutons. Combine the avocado and seafood and place in center of bowl. Cut the tomato in wedges and arrange around the edge. Add the dressing just before serving and toss lightly. Iceberg lettuce, Boston lettuce or romaine may be used for the salad greens. 6 servings.

BAKED OCEAN BAY SALAD

1 1/2 c. flaked crab meat	2 tbsp. finely chopped pimento
1 c. chopped cooked shrimp	1 tsp. Worcestershire sauce
3/4 c. salad dressing	1/2 tsp. salt
1/2 c. chopped green pepper	1/2 c. chow mein noodles
2 tbsp. finely chopped onion	Lime twists

Combine the crab meat, shrimp, salad dressing, green pepper, onion, pimento, Worcestershire sauce and salt in a bowl and mix well. Place in 1-quart casserole or 4 individual baking dishes and sprinkle with chow mein noodles. Bake at 350 degrees for 25 minutes. Garnish with lime twists. 4 servings.

Pearl Scott, Gainesville, Florida

HOT SEAFOOD SALAD

1 lge. green pepper, chopped	1 c. mayonnaise
1 sm. onion, grated	1 tsp. Worcestershire sauce
1 c. diced celery	1/2 tsp. salt
1 6 1/2-oz. can crab meat	Dash of pepper
1 can lobster	Buttered bread crumbs
2 c. cooked shrimp, halved	Paprika

Combine the green pepper, onion and celery. Drain the crab meat and lobster and chop the lobster. Combine the celery mixture, crab meat, lobster and shrimp, then chill thoroughly. Add the mayonnaise, Worcestershire sauce, salt and pepper and mix well. Turn into individual baking shells. Sprinkle with bread crumbs and paprika, then garnish with pimento strips. Bake at 350 degrees until heated through and bubbly. Serve with lemon wedges.

Mrs. Dan B. Graham, Memphis, Tennessee

TOSSED SEAFOOD SALAD

4 tbsp. salad oil	1/2 c. cooked shrimp
2 tbsp. lemon juice	1/2 c. chopped lobster
Salt and pepper to taste	1/2 c. crab meat
1 tsp. grated onion	1/2 c. sliced stuffed olives
Pinch of dry mustard	2 sm. tomatoes, chopped
1/2 c. sour cream	3 c. shredded lettuce

Combine the first 6 ingredients in a small bowl, then beat well. Combine the remaining ingredients in a salad bowl, then add the sour cream mixture and toss to mix well.

Mrs. Charles E. Howard, Port Gibson, Mississippi

CRAB DELECTABLE

1 c. crab meat	Salt and pepper to taste
1 c. chopped celery	2 tsp. vinegar
3 tomatoes, chopped	Pinch of sugar
1/2 green pepper, chopped	3 tbsp. mayonnaise
1 sm. onion, chopped	

Combine all the ingredients in a bowl, then toss to mix well. Chill thoroughly. Serve on lettuce. 6 servings.

Mrs. Carl Legett, Gulfport, Mississippi

CRAB-GRAPEFRUIT SALAD

1 lb. fresh crab meat	Mayonnaise to taste
1/2 c. French dressing	1 tsp. capers
1 can grapefruit, drained	Salt and pepper to taste

Combine the crab meat and French dressing, then chill for 2 hours. Add the remaining ingredients and blend together. Serve on lettuce.

Mrs. N. M. Maxson, Bradenton, Florida

CRAB-PEAR SALAD WITH HOT VINAIGRETTE DRESSING

1 7 1/2-oz. can Alaskan King crab	1/4 tsp. garlic powder
	1 tbsp. chopped chives
1 c. chopped celery	1/2 c. salad oil
2 hard-cooked eggs, chopped	2 tbsp. vinegar
1/4 tsp. powdered mustard	2 tbsp. fresh lemon juice
1 tsp. salt	1 1-lb. 13-oz. can pear halves
1/8 tsp. pepper	

Drain the crab and chop. Toss the crab with the celery and eggs. Blend the mustard, salt, pepper, garlic powder, chives, salad oil, vinegar and lemon juice together and bring just to a boil. Drain the pears and add the pear halves to hot liquid. Simmer for 5 minutes and remove the pears to platter. Pour the hot sauce over the crab mixture and toss lightly. Heap the crab mixture in the center of the platter. Garnish with crisp celery greens if desired. 4 servings.

Mrs. William R. Swift, Fort Lewis, Washington

CRAB LOUIS

1/4 c. minced onion	1 tsp. Worcestershire sauce
1/4 c. minced green pepper	1 tsp. prepared horseradish
2 tbsp. chopped green olives	1/4 tsp. salt
1 c. mayonnaise	1 lb. crab meat, chilled
1/4 c. chili sauce	Shredded lettuce
1 tbsp. lemon juice	

Combine all the ingredients except the crab meat and lettuce and blend thoroughly. Chill for 45 minutes. Arrange the crab on beds of lettuce, then spoon dressing over crab meat. Garnish with ripe olives, hard-boiled egg wedges, tomato wedges and lemon slices.

Mrs. Warren E. Williams, San Perlita, Texas

CRAB SALAD IN ORANGE SHELLS

4 oranges	1 tsp. grated onion
2 6 1/2-oz. cans crab meat	1/2 c. mayonnaise
1 c. minced celery	

Cut blossom end off oranges, then scoop out the pulp. Drain. Snip the cut end of orange shells into points. Drain crab meat and flake, then add orange and remaining ingredients. Stuff into orange shells. Chill thoroughly. Serve with additional mayonnaise.

Mrs. Violet Horne, Marshville, North Carolina

Dungeness Crab Salad (below)

DUNGENESS CRAB SALAD

1 lb. dungeness crab meat	1/4 c. sliced green pepper
1 15-oz. can artichoke hearts	1 tsp. salt
1 8-oz. can cut green beans	1/4 tsp. pepper
2 hard-cooked eggs, chopped	3/4 c. Thousand Island dressing
1/2 c. sliced celery	6 tomato slices
1/4 c. sliced cauliflower	6 lettuce leaves
1/4 c. sliced cucumber	Radish slices

Drain the crab meat and remove any shell or cartilage, then cut into 1/2-inch pieces. Drain the artichoke hearts and cut into fourths. Drain the green beans. Combine all the ingredients except the tomatoes, lettuce and radishes and toss lightly. Arrange a tomato slice on each lettuce leaf on salad plates and place 1 cup salad on each tomato slice. Garnish with radish slices. Serve with a thin mayonnaise dressing. 6 servings.

CRAB-WILD RICE SALAD

1 c. King crab meat	2 tbsp. vinegar
1 c. cooked wild rice	Salad greens
1/2 c. mayonnaise	2 avocados, sliced
1/4 tsp. dry mustard	

Remove any cartilage from crab and place crab in a bowl. Add the rice and toss. Blend the mayonnaise with mustard and vinegar and mix with crab mixture. Chill. Serve on salad greens and garnish with avocado. 4 servings.

Mrs. David B. Savage, Georgetown, Kentucky

HIALEAH SALAD

1/2 c. crab meat	1/4 c. Sour Cream Dressing
1/2 tsp. salt	1/2 avocado

Combine the crab meat, salt and Sour Cream Dressing thoroughly, then chill. Fill the avocado with crab mixture. Garnish with red and green pepper strips.

Sour Cream Dressing

1/4 c. sour cream	1/8 tsp. salt
1 tsp. lemon juice	Dash of pepper
1/2 tsp. vinegar	

Combine all ingredients and mix thoroughly. Chill.

Mrs. Ruth Phillips, Mt. Pleasant, South Carolina

GRAPEFRUIT-CRAB SALAD

1 1-lb. can grapefruit sections	1 c. mayonnaise or salad dressing
1 c. frozen crab meat, thawed	2 tbsp. catsup
2 tbsp. lemon juice	Hot sauce to taste
Lettuce	

Chill and drain the grapefruit. Flake the crab meat and sprinkle with 1 tablespoon lemon juice. Place grapefruit sections and crab meat on lettuce. Combine remaining lemon juice with remaining ingredients and pour over grapefruit and crab meat. 6-8 servings.

Mrs. James Osborn, El Paso, Texas

LUNCHEON CRAB SALAD

4 c. crab meat	1/3 c. minced parsley
1 1/2 c. diced celery	1 1/2 c. mayonnaise
Juice of 1 lemon	Lettuce
1 sm. onion, minced	

Remove all cartilage and shell from crab meat, then combine with the celery, lemon juice, onion, parsley and mayonnaise. Mix thoroughly but gently. Serve in lettuce cups. 6 servings.

Mrs. Gertrude Lacy, Tampa, Florida

KING CRAB IN ASPIC

2 c. cocktail vegetable juice
2 c. chili sauce
Juice of 1 lemon
2 tbsp. horseradish
6 drops of hot sauce

2 env. unflavored gelatin
1/2 c. chopped onion
1/2 c. chopped celery
1 6-oz. package frozen crab
  meat, thawed

Mix the vegetable juice, chili sauce, lemon juice, horseradish and hot sauce in a saucepan and heat through. Soften the gelatin in 1/4 cup water. Add to hot mixture and stir until dissolved. Chill until slightly thickened. Add the onion, celery and crab meat. Pour into a greased mold and chill until firm. Unmold and serve on endive, if desired. 8 servings.

Mrs. A. P. Herrewig, Raleigh, North Carolina

WEST INDIES SALAD

1 lb. crab meat
1 med. onion, chopped
1/2 c. salad oil

1/3 c. cider vinegar
1/3 c. ice water

Arrange the crab meat and onion in layers in bowl. Combine the remaining ingredients and pour over the top. Cover and refrigerate overnight. Remove from bowl with slotted spoon to serve.

Mrs. W. C. Ellis, Mobile, Alabama

NEW YEAR'S HERRING SALAD

1 8-oz. jar herring tidbits
  in wine sauce
Lemon juice
3 apples, diced
2 to 3 tsp. sugar (opt.)

1 celery heart
3/4 jar harvard beets
1 c. mayonnaise
Lettuce

Drain the herring tidbits and cut in small pieces. Place in a mixing bowl. Sprinkle lemon juice over apples and add sugar. Add to the herring and mix. Grate the celery heart and stir into herring mixture. Add the beets and mayonnaise and toss. Refrigerate for 1 hour. Serve on lettuce.

Mrs. Ridgely D. Miller, Anniston, Alabama

PONTE VEDRA LOBSTER SALAD

1 1/2 c. diced cooked lobster
1/4 c. lime juice
1/2 c. chopped celery
1 tsp. salt
1/4 tsp. pepper

Mayonnaise
Lettuce cups or avocado
  halves
2 tbsp. capers

Combine the lobster and lime juice and chill for at least 3 hours. Add the celery, salt, pepper and enough mayonnaise to moisten. Toss lightly. Serve in lettuce cups. Sprinkle with capers. Garnish with hard-boiled egg halves and ripe olives. 4 servings.

Mrs. Esther Blaylock, Marathon, Florida

APPLE-LOBSTER BUFFET MOLD

2 10-oz. packages frozen lobster-tails, cooked	3 env. unflavored gelatin
	3 chicken bouillon cubes
1 1/2 c. diced Washington State apples	3/4 tsp. dill salt
	1 10-oz. package frozen broccoli, cooked
1/2 c. chopped cucumber	
1/2 c. chopped celery	1 sliced Washington State apple
2 tbsp. chopped pimento	
1 tsp. grated onion	Salad greens
2 tbsp. lemon juice	3 hard-cooked eggs

Drain the lobster, then remove the meat from shells and cut into bite-sized chunks. Combine with the diced apple, cucumber, celery, pimento, onion and lemon juice. Cover and chill. Soften the gelatin in 1 cup cold water. Dissolve the bouillon cubes in 2 1/2 cups boiling water, then add the dill salt. Add the gelatin and stir until thoroughly dissolved. Add 1 1/2 cups cold water to gelatin mixture and chill until thickened. Arrange the cooked broccoli in the bottom of 12-cup mold, then intersperse with the apple slices. Spoon 1/2 cup of the gelatin over broccoli and apples and chill until firm. Combine lobster mixture with remaining gelatin and pour over first layer. Chill until firm. Unmold on salad platter lined with salad greens. Garnish with wedges of hard-cooked eggs, parsley and additional apple slices. Serve with mayonnaise and caper dressing. 8-10 servings.

Apple-Lobster Buffet Mold (above)

FLORIDA LOBSTER-POTATO SALAD

2 c. diced cooked lobster	2 hard-boiled eggs, chopped
2 c. diced cooked potatoes	1/2 c. mayonnaise
1/4 c. chopped onions	Salt and pepper to taste

Combine all the ingredients in a large salad bowl and blend lightly. Serve on lettuce with saltines. 6 servings.

Sally Knox, Miami, Florida

LOBSTER IN CUCUMBER SHELLS

1/2 sm. onion, grated	10 7 to 8-in. cucumbers
Juice of 1 lime	1 1/2 lb. cooked lobster, diced
2 1/4 c. mayonnaise	3/4 c. minced celery
3/4 c. chili sauce	3 tbsp. minced parsley
Salt and pepper to taste	3 tbsp. minced dill
Cayenne pepper to taste	

Place the onion in a bowl. Add the lime juice, mayonnaise and chili sauce and mix well. Season with salt, pepper and cayenne pepper. Peel the cucumbers and cut into halves. Remove pulp from cucumbers to make boat-shaped shells. Mix the lobster, celery and 1 cup mayonnaise mixture and place in cucumber boats. Mix the parsley and dill and sprinkle on lobster mixture. Chill. Serve on lettuce with remaining mayonnaise mixture.

Mrs. Anne Cunningham, Ft. Walton, Florida

LANGOUSTE DE MER

4 c. cooked cubed lobster	1 tsp. grated onion
4 hard-cooked eggs, chopped	1 tsp. Worcestershire sauce
1/2 c. diced celery	1/2 tsp. salt
1/4 c. minced parsley	1 c. mayonnaise
1 tsp. dry mustard	

Combine the lobster, eggs, celery and parsley, then add the mustard, onion, Worcestershire sauce and salt, tossing to blend. Add the mayonnaise and mix well. Serve on lettuce. 6 servings.

Mrs. Emily Porter, Savoy, Texas

LOBSTER SALAD IN PINEAPPLE SHELLS

1 pineapple	1/2 c. chopped green mango
2 c. sour cream	chutney
2 tbsp. lemon juice	4 c. chopped cooked lobster
1 tsp. salt	1 c. sliced pimento-stuffed olives
1 tbsp. curry powder	1/2 c. toasted almonds

Cut the pineapple and crown in half lengthwise, leaving the crown on the pineapple, then carefully cut out the fruit in wedges, leaving a 1/2-inch shell. Remove the core and cut the fruit into 1 1/2-inch wedges. Blend the sour cream, lemon juice, salt, curry powder and chutney together and toss lightly with the lobster, olives and pineapple wedges. Heap the lobster mixture into the pineapple shells and sprinkle with the almonds. Yield: 6 servings.

Mrs. Allen Goodson, Fort Hood, Texas

LOBSTER ASPIC PARISIAN

3 env. unflavored gelatin	1 1/2 c. cooked peas
1 1/3 c. cold water	1 c. diced cooked carrots
2 cans bouillon, heated	1 1/2 c. diced cooked potatoes
2 tbsp. lemon juice	2 tsp. salt
2 tsp. Worcestershire sauce	2/3 c. mayonnaise
1 1/2 lb. cooked lobster chunks	

Soften the gelatin in water and dissolve in bouillon. Add the lemon juice and Worcestershire sauce and chill until thickened. Pour 1 cup gelatin mixture into 4-cup mold. Arrange half the lobster in gelatin mixture and chill until firm. Dice remaining lobster. Add the peas, carrots, potatoes, salt and mayonnaise and mix well. Stir in remaining gelatin mixture and pour over firm gelatin. Chill until firm. Unmold onto lettuce and garnish with tomato wedges and ripe olives. 8-10 servings.

Mrs. C. Miller, Birmingham, Alabama

CHILLED SALMON MOLD WITH CUCUMBER SAUCE

2 c. canned salmon	2 egg yolks, beaten
1/2 tbsp. salt	1 1/2 tbsp. butter
1 1/2 tbsp. sugar	3/4 c. milk
1 1/2 tsp. flour	1/4 c. vinegar
1 tsp. dry mustard	3/4 tbsp. unflavored gelatin

Remove the skin and bones from the salmon and flake. Combine the salt, sugar, flour and mustard in top of double boiler, then add the egg yolks, butter, milk and vinegar and mix. Cook over hot water, stirring constantly, until thickened. Soften the gelatin in 2 tablespoons water, then stir into the hot mixture. Cool thoroughly, then add the salmon. Pour into a mold and chill until firm. Unmold on a large platter. Garnish with lettuce, cucumbers and stuffed eggs.

Cucumber Sauce

1 cucumber	2 tbsp. vinegar
1/2 c. heavy cream	1/4 tsp. salt

Peel, chop and drain the cucumber thoroughly, then chill. Beat the cream until thick, then add the vinegar gradually, beating until fluffy. Fold in the salt and cucumber. Serve with salmon mold.

Alice Cox, Vanceburg, Kentucky

Salmon Steaks in Aspic (below)

SALMON STEAKS IN ASPIC

6 salmon steaks, 1 in. thick	1 stalk celery, chopped
6 peppercorns	1 med. carrot, sliced
1 tbsp. salt	2 env. unflavored gelatin
1 tsp. dillweed	1/2 c. fresh lemon juice
1 sm. onion, sliced	

Place the salmon in a 12-inch frypan, then sprinkle with the peppercorns, salt and dillweed. Add the onion, celery and carrot, then pour 4 cups boiling water over all. Cover and bring to a boil, then simmer for 5 to 10 minutes or until fish flakes easily when tested with a fork. Do not overcook. Cool the salmon in the liquid, then carefully remove the skin and bone. Chill thoroughly. Heat the fish stock and strain. Soften the gelatin in the lemon juice, then add to the hot strained stock and stir until the gelatin is dissolved. Refrigerate until thickened. Pour half the gelatin mixture into a 13 x 9 x 2-inch baking dish, then arrange the salmon steaks in the dish. Spoon the remaining gelatin mixture over the steaks. Chill until firm. Cut around each salmon steak, leaving a border of gelatin, and arrange on a large, lettuce-lined platter. Garnish with fresh dill sprigs, deviled egg halves, radish roses and ripe olives. Serve with a mayonnaise or seafood sauce. 6 servings.

RIPAILLE SALMON SALAD

2 env. unflavored gelatin	1 tsp. salt
2 sm. packages cream cheese	1 sm. onion, grated
1 can mushroom soup	1 c. chopped celery
1 tsp. Worcestershire sauce	1 lge. can red salmon,
1 c. mayonnaise	drained and flaked

Soften the gelatin in 1/4 cup water in top of double boiler, then dissolve over hot water. Stir in the cream cheese until melted. Remove from heat and add the remaining ingredients. Mix well, then turn in mold. Chill until firm.

Mrs. W. Elmer Skidmore, Paris, Texas

GOURMET SALMON-CUCUMBER SALAD

1/2 c. sugar	1 1-lb. can salmon
1 tsp. dry mustard	1 med. cucumber, diced
1 tsp. salt	4 stalks celery, chopped
1 1/4 tsp. monosodium glutamate	1/4 c. mayonnaise
4 1/2 tbsp. cider vinegar	2 tbsp. lemon juice
4 tsp. grated onion	1 to 2 tbsp. capers
1 c. salad oil	Dash of pepper
1 tbsp. celery seed	

Mix the sugar, mustard, salt and 1/4 teaspoon monosodium glutamate, then stir in 2 tablespoons cider vinegar and 1 teaspoon onion. Add the salad oil gradually, beating constantly until thick and light. Beat in the remaining vinegar and celery seed. Drain the salmon and remove skin and bones, then flake. Add the remaining ingredients and mix well. Chill thoroughly. Pile lightly on a serving platter. Garnish with melon balls and watercress and serve with the dressing. 4-6 servings.

Eugenia Aull, Richmond, Virginia

SALMON MOUSSE WITH AVOCADO CREAM

1 pkg. unflavored gelatin	1 tsp. grated onion
1 c. water	1 tsp. prepared horseradish
1 bouillon cube	1 c. chopped ripe olives
1 tsp. salt	1 lge. can salmon
2 tbsp. vinegar	1 c. mayonnaise
2 tbsp. lemon juice	

Soften the gelatin in 1/4 cup water. Place remaining water and bouillon cube in a saucepan and heat, stirring constantly, until bouillon cube is dissolved. Add the gelatin and stir until dissolved. Blend in the salt, vinegar, lemon juice, onion, horseradish and olives. Drain the salmon and remove bones. Flake the salmon and add to gelatin mixture. Blend in mayonnaise and pour into a mold. Chill until firm, then unmold.

Avocado Cream

1 c. mashed avocado	3/4 tsp. salt
1/2 c. sour cream	Dash of hot sauce

Blend all ingredients until smooth and spread over salmon mold. Garnish with salad greens, tomato wedges and cucumber sticks. 4 servings.

Mabel Byrd Francis, Miami, Florida

MOLDED SALMON MOLD

1 pkg. lime gelatin	1/2 c. mayonnaise
1 3/4 c. boiling water	1 c. chopped celery
3 tbsp. vinegar	1 c. diced cucumber
1/4 tsp. salt	1 tall can red salmon,
1 tsp. sugar	flaked
1/4 tsp. dry mustard	

Dissolve the gelatin in boiling water, then add the vinegar. Chill until thickened. Combine the salt, sugar, mustard and mayonnaise and fold into the gelatin mixture. Add the remaining ingredients and pour into cold water-rinsed molds. Chill until firm. Serve on lettuce and garnish with pimento. 8 servings.

Mrs. Ann Click McGaughy, Calera, Alabama

MACKEREL SALAD

1 can mackerel	1 onion, minced
3 cooked potatoes, mashed	1 tsp. sugar
2 c. crushed crackers	3 hard-boiled eggs, chopped
1/2 c. vinegar	

Rinse the mackerel with cold water, then drain. Place in bowl, then add the remaining ingredients. Mix well, then chill for about 2 hours before serving.

Mrs. E. V. Hill, Corbin, Kentucky

OYSTER SALAD

1 5-oz. can oysters	3 pimentos, minced
Crackers	1/2 c. finely chopped celery
6 sweet pickles, diced	Salt to taste
6 hard-cooked eggs, diced	Mayonnaise

Pour the oysters in a bowl, then add enough crumbled crackers to absorb the juice. Add the pickles, eggs, pimentos, celery, salt and enough mayonnaise to moisten. Mix until well blended.

Mrs. Osbern Harkey, Plainview, Arkansas

SARDINE SALAD

4 med. sardines	Lettuce leaves
2 hard-cooked eggs, quartered	1/4 c. mayonnaise

Drain the sardines and cut each into 4 pieces. Place the sardines and eggs on lettuce and top with mayonnaise.

Mrs. Hollis Corbin, Birmingham, Alabama

SCALLOP SALAD

2 lb. cooked scallops
1 c. sliced celery
1 c. diced cucumbers
1/4 c. sliced stuffed olives
1/2 c. French dressing

1 c. mayonnaise
Salt to taste
Lemon juice to taste
Watercress

Cut the scallops into chunks and place in a bowl. Add the celery, cucumbers, olives and French dressing and mix well. Chill for several hours. Add the mayonnaise, salt and lemon juice and mix well. Serve on watercress in scallop shells. 6 servings.

Sharon Hernandez, New Braunfels, Texas

SEAFOOD SALAD

1 pkg. herbed or risotta rice
1 can shrimp, drained

1 can crab meat, drained
Oil and vinegar dressing

Cook the rice according to package directions, then chill thoroughly. Place in salad bowl and fold in the shrimp and crab meat. Toss lightly with the dressing. Garnish with cucumber slices and additional shrimp, if desired.

Seafood Salad (above)

CITRUS-AVOCADO SHRIMP MOLD

2 env. unflavored gelatin	1 c. heavy cream, whipped
1/2 c. grapefruit juice	Lettuce
1 c. mayonnaise	Grapefruit sections
1/2 tsp. salt	Sliced avocado
1 1/2 c. mashed avocado	1 lb. cooked shrimp, deveined

Soften the gelatin in 1/2 cup water in a saucepan. Place over low heat and stir until gelatin is dissolved. Add the grapefruit juice, then chill until thickened. Add the mayonnaise, salt and avocado, then fold in the whipped cream. Turn into a mold and chill until firm. Unmold onto a lettuce-lined platter. Surround with grapefruit, avocado and shrimp.

Mrs. Russell Baker, Atlanta, Georgia

LIME-SHRIMP MOLD

1 No. 2 can crushed pineapple	1 c. cottage cheese
1 6-oz. package lime gelatin	2 c. fresh cooked shrimp

Drain the pineapple and reserve 1/2 cup juice. Dissolve the gelatin in 2 cups hot water, then add 1 1/2 cups cold water and the reserved pineapple juice. Chill until thickened. Add the pineapple and cottage cheese and mix well, then fold in the shrimp. Turn into a mold and chill until firm. 8-10 servings.

Mrs. Elizabeth S. Richardson, Orangeburg, South Carolina

PALM BEACH SALAD

2 c. diced avocado	1 c. chili sauce
Lemon juice	1/2 c. mayonnaise
1 c. chopped celery	6 slices cooked bacon,
24 boiled cleaned shrimp	crumbled
1 tbsp. minced chives	

Sprinkle avocado with lemon juice. Add remaining ingredients except bacon and mix. Chill. Serve on lettuce leaves and garnish with bacon. 6 servings.

Freda Avant Jay, West Palm Beach, Florida

CURRIED SHRIMP SALAD

1 1/3 c. instant rice	3/4 tsp. curry powder
1/2 tsp. salt	1 tbsp. grated onion
1 1/3 c. boiling water	1 c. cooked shrimp, diced
3/4 c. mayonnaise	1 c. chopped celery
1 1/2 tsp. lemon juice	

Combine the rice, salt and water in a saucepan, then bring to a boil. Cover and remove from heat, then let stand for 5 minutes. Uncover and cool to room temperature. Combine the mayonnaise, lemon juice, curry powder and onion and mix well. Combine the shrimp and celery and stir into the mayonnaise mixture. Add the rice and mix lightly. Chill for 1 hour.

Marlene Cloud, Dalton, Georgia

GEORGIA SHRIMP SALAD

2 cans frozen grapefruit sections	1/2 c. chopped pecans
1 sm. package cream cheese, softened	2 tbsp. minced onion
1/3 c. mayonnaise	1 1/2 lb. cooked shrimp, cleaned
1/2 c. catsup	Lettuce cups

Thaw and drain the grapefruit. Blend the cream cheese and mayonnaise together until smooth. Add the catsup, pecans and onion and mix thoroughly. Stir in the shrimp. Place lettuce cups on salad plates and arrange the grapefruit in cups. Spoon the shrimp mixture over the top. 4 servings.

Mrs. Malcom D. Cameron, Snook, Texas

SAN BLAS SHRIMP

2 3-oz. packages cream cheese	2 cans shrimp, drained
1 can tomato soup	1 c. chopped celery
2 env. unflavored gelatin	1 c. chopped green pepper
1 c. mayonnaise	1 c. chopped onion
	1 c. chopped sweet pickle

Combine the cream cheese and soup in a saucepan and simmer, stirring, until the cream cheese is melted. Soften the gelatin in 1/2 cup water, then stir into the hot soup mixture. Chill until thickened. Combine remaining ingredients and fold into the gelatin mixture. Turn into a mold, then chill until firm.

Mrs. Jack Arnall, Houston, Texas

ST. REGIS SHRIMP SALAD

1/2 c. French dressing	1/4 c. chopped green pepper
1/4 tsp. curry powder	2 hard-boiled egg yolks, sieved
1 c. cooked shrimp	
1/4 c. crushed pineapple	

Combine the dressing and curry powder, then add the shrimp and marinate in refrigerator for at least 3 hours. Add the pineapple, green pepper and egg yolks. Serve on cabbage leaf and garnish with mayonnaise and capers.

Mrs. Lucille F. Snow, Roanoke, Virginia

MANDARIN SHRIMP SALAD

1 5 1/4-oz. can water chestnuts	Salt and white pepper to taste
1 11-oz. can mandarin oranges	Lettuce leaves
1/3 c. heavy cream, whipped	1 bunch watercress
1/2 c. mayonnaise	1 2-oz. jar pimento strips,
2 lb. boiled cleaned shrimp	drained
2 dashes of hot sauce	

Drain and slice the water chestnuts. Drain the oranges. Fold the whipped cream into mayonnaise. Stir in the shrimp, water chestnuts, oranges, hot sauce, salt and pepper and marinate in refrigerator for 30 minutes. Spoon onto lettuce and garnish with watercress and pimento strips. 4 servings.

Mrs. R. C. Graham, Columbia, South Carolina

APPLE-TUNA MOUSSE

1 3-oz. package lemon-lime	1 tbsp. fresh lemon juice
flavored gelatin	1 7-oz. can tuna, drained
1 c. boiling water	1 c. chopped Washington State
1/4 tsp. salt	apples
Pepper to taste	1/2 c. sliced ripe olives
2/3 c. evaporated milk	2 tbsp. chopped chives

Place the gelatin in a medium mixing bowl, then add the boiling water, salt and pepper and stir until gelatin is dissolved. Chill in refrigerator until thickened. Chill the evaporated milk in an ice cube tray until ice crystals form around the edge. Whip the milk until stiff and peaks form. Add the lemon juice to the milk and blend. Add the tuna, apples, olives and chives to the gelatin, then fold in the milk. Turn into a fish-shaped mold and chill until set. Unmold on salad greens and garnish with thin apple slices and olive slices. 6 servings.

Photograph for this recipe on page 32.

TUNA-AVOCADO MOLD

2 env. unflavored gelatin	1 tsp. sugar
1/2 tsp. salt	1 c. mashed avocado
5 tbsp. lemon juice	1/2 c. mayonnaise
1 can drained tuna, flaked	1/2 c. sour cream
1 c. chopped celery	Dash of hot sauce

Soften 1 envelope of gelatin in 1/4 cup water, then add 1 cup hot water and stir until gelatin is dissolved. Add the salt and 3 tablespoons lemon juice, then chill until partially set. Fold the tuna and the celery into the gelatin mixture. Pour into a loaf pan and chill until set. Soften the remaining gelatin in 3/4 cup water, then dissolve over hot water. Add the sugar and remaining lemon juice. Chill until thickened. Fold in the avocado, mayonnaise, sour cream and hot sauce. Pour over set layer. Chill until firm. Unmold and serve.

Mrs. Guy H. Orr, Birmingham, Alabama

Oriental Tuna-Apple Salad (below)

ORIENTAL TUNA-APPLE SALAD

1 med. head lettuce	1 1/2 tsp. soy sauce
2 Washington State apples	1 tsp. lemon juice
1 c. mandarin oranges	1/4 c. mayonnaise
1 5-oz. can water chestnuts	1/4 tsp. celery salt
1 6 1/2-oz. can tuna,	1/4 tsp. onion salt
drained	1/4 tsp. orange peel

Break the lettuce into bite-sized pieces into a large bowl. Core the apples, then dice. Drain the oranges and slice the chestnuts. Combine the apples, oranges, water chestnuts and tuna chunks. Toss gently with the lettuce. Combine the remaining ingredients and pour over salad, then toss again and serve immediately. 8 servings.

SEAFOAM SALAD

1 pkg. lime gelatin	1 can tuna, drained
2 tbsp. mayonnaise	1 c. chopped celery

Prepare the gelatin according to package directions, then add remaining ingredients. Pour into mold and chill until firm. Serve with crackers or chips. 6 servings.

Annette James, Lebanon, Tennessee

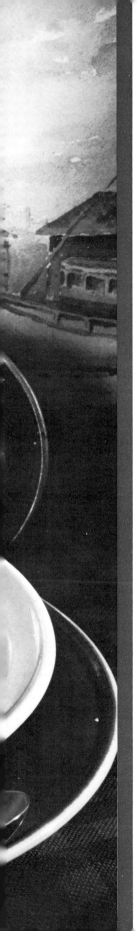

seafood soups and chowders

This chapter on seafood soups and chowders (stews, gumbos, and bisques as well!) will introduce you to a number of uniquely satisfying and wholly appetizing foods. And because seafood is the major ingredient in all these recipes, the soups and chowders you prepare will also be healthful and nutritious.

All the recipes in this section share several features in common: they are liquid; they usually contain an assortment of vegetables; and they are simmered for many hours to develop a fine mellow flavor.

Several of these recipes consist of milk or cream and seafood, delicately blended with herbs and finely chopped onion. Although many varieties of fish are used, the distinctively sweet taste of shellfish, in particular, excels in these rich mixtures. Both Oyster-Onion Stew and Clam-Corn Chowder are rich with the protein of shellfish and the wholesome goodness of milk.

Vegetable-rich and seafood-combination soups are also included in this chapter. Original Maryland Crab Soup is loaded with fresh steamed hard-shell crabs and vegetables: cabbage, carrots, celery, green beans, lima beans, and corn. Others like Bouillabaisse and Potpourri Chowder are tomato-based.

You will enjoy preparing many of the recipes in the following chapter.

Seafood Gumbo (below)

SEAFOOD GUMBO

1/2 lb. fish fillets	2/3 c. sliced okra
1 1/2 c. chicken broth	2/3 c. diced carrots
1 c. clam broth	1/4 c. chopped onion
1 7-oz. can crab meat	Salt and pepper to taste
2 tomatoes, chopped	3 c. hot cooked rice

Cut the fish into 1-inch pieces, then combine all the ingredients except the salt, pepper and rice. Bring to a boil, then cover and simmer for 15 to 20 minutes. Season with salt and pepper. Serve in bowls, then top with scoops of rice. 6-8 servings.

CALIFORNIA BOUILLABAISSE

2 lb. halibut steaks	1 lb. shrimp, deveined
1 carrot	1 c. oysters and liquor
1 bay leaf	1 1-lb. can tomatoes, cut up
2 tsp. salt	1 tbsp. lemon juice
1/4 tsp. pepper	1 2/3 c. canned pitted
2 med. onions, sliced	California ripe olives
3 tbsp. olive oil	2 tbsp. chopped parsley
1/4 c. flour	

Cut the halibut into large pieces and remove the skin and bones. Combine the carrot, 4 cups water, bay leaf, salt and pepper in a large saucepan and bring to a boil. Add the halibut, then reduce the heat and simmer for 10 minutes. Remove the halibut, carrot and bay leaf. Cook the onions in oil until tender but not browned, then stir in the flour. Strain the stock and stir into the onion mixture gradually. Cool until thickened, stirring occasionally. Add the shrimp and cook slowly for 5 minutes. Add the oysters, tomatoes, lemon juice, olives and halibut and simmer for 5 minutes. Add the parsley just before serving. 3 quarts.

Photograph for this recipe on page 52.

LAST MINUTE SEAFOOD BISQUE

1 can clam chowder	1 c. cleaned cooked shrimp
1 2/3 c. evaporated milk	1 c. minced clams
1 3-oz. can broiled chopped	1/4 c. cooking sherry
mushrooms	Butter
1 c. flaked crab meat	

Combine the chowder and milk in a saucepan, then bring to a boil. Reduce the heat, then add the mushrooms and liquid, crab meat, shrimp and clams and heat through. Stir in sherry just before serving. Serve in soup bowls, then dot with butter and garnish with parsley. 4-5 servings.

Mrs. Frances Gibson, Jackson, Mississippi

STOCKPOT GUMBO

1/2 c. butter	1 lge. bay leaf
1 lb. fresh okra, thinly	1/2 tsp. thyme
sliced	2 tsp. salt
1/2 c. finely chopped onion	Freshly ground pepper to
1/2 c. finely chopped green	taste
pepper	1 lb. small fresh shrimp
1/2 tsp. minced garlic	1/2 lb. lump crab meat
2 tbsp. flour	16 oysters
4 c. chicken stock	2 tsp. lemon juice
2 c. chopped fresh tomatoes	2 tsp. Worcestershire sauce
6 sprigs of parsley	1/4 tsp. hot sauce

Melt 4 tablespoons of the butter in a 12-inch frying pan over moderate heat. Add the okra and cook, stirring constantly, until okra stops roping or white threads disappear. Melt the remaining butter in a heavy 2 or 3-quart soup pot over moderate heat. Add the onion, green pepper and garlic and saute lightly for about 5 minutes. Stir in the flour and cook for 2 to 3 minutes longer, stirring constantly. Stir in the chicken stock slowly, then add the okra, tomatoes, parsley, thyme, salt and pepper. Bring to a boil, then reduce heat and simmer, partially covered, for 30 minutes. Shell and devein the shrimp, then add to the tomato mixture and simmer for 5 minutes. Add crab meat and oysters and simmer for 2 to 3 minutes or until oysters curl around edges and crab meat is heated through. Season with the lemon juice, Worcestershire sauce and hot sauce. Serve the gumbo over small mounds rice in deep soup plates. 8-10 servings.

Mrs. R. A. Jewell, Amarillo, Texas

FISH AND CRAB CHOWDER

1/4 c. butter	2 bay leaves
1/2 c. chopped onions	1/2 lb. frozen haddock
2 chicken bouillon cubes	fillets
2 c. hot water	4 c. milk
1 c. chopped celery	1/3 c. flour
3 peeled carrots, chopped	1 6 1/2-oz. can crab meat,
1 tsp. salt	flaked
1/8 tsp. pepper	

Melt the butter in a large heavy saucepan over low heat, then add the onions and saute until tender. Dissolve the bouillon cubes in the water, then add to onions. Add the celery, carrots, salt, pepper and bay leaves. Cut the haddock into bite-sized pieces and add to onion mixture. Simmer for about 30 minutes or until vegetables are tender. Add 1 cup milk gradually to the flour, then stir into the soup. Stir in the remaining milk. Cook, stirring constantly, until thickened. Stir in the crab meat. Serve in large bowls and garnish with parsley sprigs. 6-8 servings.

Mrs. Effie North, Arlington, Virginia

POTPOURRI CHOWDER

1 can oysters with juice	1 1/2 qt. milk
1 tbsp. flour	1/2 c. cream
1 can clam chowder	Salt and pepper to taste
1 can shrimp, drained	Chopped green onions

Pour the oysters into a large Dutch oven, then stir in the flour. Cook, stirring, for 3 minutes. Add the clam chowder, shrimp, milk and cream. Season with salt and pepper and simmer until heated through. Serve in soup bowls, then sprinkle with green onions. 6 servings.

Mrs. Laura Harvey, Ocala, Florida

SEAFOOD BISQUE

1 4-oz. can crab meat	1 tsp. salt
1 4-oz. can lobster	Dash of pepper
1 sm. onion, minced	1/8 tsp. celery salt
2 tbsp. butter	1 c. water
2 tbsp. flour	3 c. milk

Drain the crab meat and lobster and reserve the liquid. Saute the onion in butter in a 2-quart saucepan until transparent, then stir in the flour, salt, pepper and celery salt. Cook, stirring constantly, until well blended and bubbling. Remove from heat, then stir in the water and milk gradually. Bring to a boil and boil for 1 minute, stirring constantly. Cut the lobster into small pieces and flake the crab meat, then stir into the hot mixture. Add the reserved liquid and heat to serving temperature. Serve with saltines or oyster crackers, if desired. 4 servings.

Mrs. Charles Mathews, Lexington, Kentucky

CLAM-CORN CHOWDER

2 c. diced potatoes
2 c. water
2 8-oz. cans minced
  clams
1 12-oz. can Shoe Peg corn
4 hard-cooked eggs, chopped

2 tsp. salt
1/8 tsp. pepper
2 tbsp. butter or margarine
1/2 tsp. Worcestershire
  sauce
2 tbsp. chopped parsley

Combine the potatoes and water in a saucepan and cook until soft. Add the remaining ingredients, then bring to a boil. Reduce the heat and simmer for 3 minutes. 6-8 servings.

Mrs. Lois Johnston, Dover, Delaware

CLAM-TOMATO CHOWDER

2/3 c. diced celery
6 sm. potatoes, diced
3 carrots, shredded
4 slices bacon, diced
1 onion, diced

Salt and pepper to taste
1 pt. clams
1 lge. can tomatoes, sieved
Pinch of thyme
1 can evaporated milk

Combine the celery, potatoes and carrots in large saucepan, then add 2 cups water. Cook, covered, until vegetables are tender. Fry the bacon and onion together until bacon is crisp, then add to the vegetables. Season with salt and pepper. Add the clams, tomatoes and thyme, then simmer for 10 to 15 minutes. Add the milk just before serving and heat through.

Mrs. Betty Waites, Tuscaloosa, Alabama

RUTTLAND CLAM CHOWDER

2 doz. large clams
1/2 c. cornmeal
1/4 lb. salt pork, diced
2 lge. onions, chopped
1 carrot, diced
1 c. chopped celery

1 green pepper, diced
2 c. chopped tomatoes
2 potatoes, diced
Dash of thyme
Salt and pepper to taste
Flour

Wash the clams thoroughly and scrub the shells. Cover with salted water and add the cornmeal. Let stand for 3 hours. Place the clams in a kettle, then add a small amount of water. Cover and steam until the clams open. Remove the clams and reserve the liquor. Cool the clams, then mince. Fry the salt pork until brown, then remove the pork pieces and add the onions, carrot, celery and green pepper to the drippings. Brown lightly, then add the tomatoes, potatoes, 4 cups water, clams, reserved liquor and seasonings. Cook until the vegetables are tender. Thicken slightly with a flour paste, if desired.

Mrs. G. N. Rogers, Richmond, Virginia

COD CHOWDER

1 c. diced onion	1/2 tsp. basil
1 c. diced celery	1/4 tsp. pepper
5 slices bacon, diced	1 1-lb. package frozen cod
4 c. diced potatoes	1 No. 303 can corn
2 tsp. salt	1 lge. can evaporated milk

Combine the onion, celery and bacon in a skillet and saute until lightly browned. Drain off excess fat. Combine the potatoes, salt, basil, pepper and 2 cups water in a kettle, then simmer, covered, for 15 minutes. Cut the cod into 1-inch pieces, then add to the potato mixture. Cover and simmer for 15 minutes longer. Stir in the corn, milk and bacon mixture and simmer until heated through, adding water if needed. 10-12 servings.

Mrs. Janice Hearn, Baltimore, Maryland

COURT BOUILLON

1 1/2 lb. catfish	Sugar to taste
Salt and pepper to taste	3 pt. water
1 clove of garlic, minced	Pinch of oregano
1/4 c. cooking oil	Pinch of thyme
1/3 c. flour	1/2 lemon, sliced
1 med. onion, minced	1 tbsp. chopped parsley
1 stalk celery, chopped	1 tbsp. chopped green onion
3/4 c. chopped tomatoes	tops
2 tbsp. tomato sauce	3 tbsp. sherry
1 bay leaf	

Cut the catfish into small serving pieces, then season with salt, pepper and garlic. Place in a dish, then cover and chill for several hours. Heat the oil in a large heavy pot, then stir in the flour and cook, stirring constantly, until browned. Add the onion and celery and cook, stirring constantly, for about 5 minutes. Add the tomatoes, tomato sauce, bay leaf, sugar and water and stir until the tomato mixture comes to a hard boil. Reduce heat to low and cover with tight lid, then simmer for 45 minutes. Add catfish, oregano, thyme and lemon and simmer for 20 minutes longer. Add the parsley, green onion tops and sherry and cook for 1 minute longer. Serve over hot rice in soup plates and garnish with lemon.

Mrs. Marvin Needham, Lafayette, Louisiana

BALTIMORE CRAB SOUP

2 tbsp. butter	1/4 c. chopped celery
1 onion, finely chopped	1 tbsp. chopped parsley
1 tbsp. flour	Dash of hot sauce
1 c. crab meat	3 c. scalded milk

Melt the butter in a large saucepan, then add the onion and saute until lightly browned. Stir in the flour, then stir in 2 cups warm water slowly and cook until slightly thickened. Add the crab meat, celery, parsley and seasonings and simmer for 30 minutes. Add the milk just before serving. 6 servings.

Mrs. Oliver Kjelland, Temple, Texas

CRAB BISQUE

2 cans tomato soup	**2 c. crab meat**
1 can split pea soup	**1/3 c. sherry**
1 c. milk	

Combine the soups and the milk in a saucepan and simmer for 20 minutes. Add the crab meat and simmer until heated through. Stir in the sherry just before serving. 5 servings.

Mrs. Evelyn Jason, Jacksonville, Florida

CHILLED CURRIED CRAB BISQUE

1/4 c. butter	**1 7 1/2-oz. can crab meat**
1/3 c. chopped celery	**1 tbsp. lemon juice**
3 tbsp. flour	**1 1/2 tsp. curry powder**
1 tsp. salt	**1/2 c. whipping cream**
1 qt. milk	

Melt the butter in a saucepan over low heat, then add the celery and cook until tender. Blend in the flour and salt. Add the milk and cook, stirring constantly, until sauce is smooth and thickened. Cool. Drain and flake the crab meat, then add the crab meat, lemon juice, curry powder and whipping cream to the celery mixture, stirring until well blended. Chill thoroughly, then serve in chilled bowls. Garnish with watercress, if desired. 6-8 servings.

Chilled Curried Crab Bisque (above)

CRAB SOUP

1 can tomato soup	1/4 lb. mushrooms, sliced
1 can mushroom soup	Butter
1 can pea soup	3/4 lb. fresh crab meat
3 c. half and half	1/4 c. sherry

Combine the soups and half and half in a saucepan. Blend until smooth, then simmer, stirring constantly, until heated through. Saute the mushrooms in a small amount of butter, then stir into the soup mixture. Add the crab meat and sherry and bring almost to a boil, stirring constantly. Serve immediately.

Mrs. Norma Bowman, Savannah, Georgia

DAUPHIN ISLAND CRAB GUMBO

2 c. finely chopped celery	2 c. canned tomatoes
2 c. finely chopped onions	1 c. sliced okra
1 green pepper, finely chopped	1/2 tsp. salt
1 tbsp. minced parsley	1/4 tsp. pepper
3 tbsp. bacon drippings	1/4 tsp. chili powder
3/4 c. sifted flour	Hot sauce to taste
2 c. crab meat	1 tbsp. gumbo file

Saute the celery, onions, green pepper and parsley in the drippings in a skillet until soft, then remove the vegetables with a slotted spoon and place in a kettle. Brown the flour slowly in the drippings, then add to the vegetables. Add 3 quarts water and the crab and cook for 30 minutes. Add the tomatoes, okra, salt, pepper, chili powder and hot sauce, then simmer for 1 hour. Remove from heat and stir in the file. Serve over rice. 6-8 servings.

Mrs. C. F. Wilson, Mobile, Alabama

ORIGINAL MARYLAND CRAB SOUP

6 steamed hard-shelled crabs	2 carrots, diced
1/2 lb. slab bacon, quartered	1 c. finely shredded cabbage
3 tomatoes, quartered	1/4 c. chopped parsley
3 potatoes, diced	2 tbsp. flour
1 med. onion, diced	1 tsp. mustard
1 c. frozen whole kernel corn	1/4 c. melted butter or margarine
1 c. frozen lima beans	1 tbsp. Worcestershire sauce
1 c. frozen green beans	
2 stalks celery, diced	

Break the claws off the crabs and discard the small claws, then crack the large claws. Pull off the back shell and remove the gills and face of crab. Break crab in half and cut across each half parallel to shell. Do not remove the meat. Combine the crabs, bacon and 3 quarts water in a kettle and simmer for 1 hour. Remove the bacon. Add the vegetables and simmer until vegetables are just tender. Blend the flour and the mustard into the butter, then add the Worcestershire sauce. Stir into the soup mixture and simmer for 5 minutes longer. 12 servings.

Mrs. Fred S. Thomas, Kingsville, Maryland

SHE-CRAB SOUP

1 can cream of mushroom soup	Salt and pepper to taste
1 can cream of asparagus soup	2 c. crab meat
1 c. half and half	1/4 c. sherry
1 can evaporated milk	

Place the soups in a 3-quart saucepan, then blend in the half and half and milk. Add the salt, pepper and crab meat, then, simmer, stirring constantly, until heated through. Do not boil. Remove from heat and stir in the sherry. Serve immediately. 4-6 servings.

Mrs. James F. Coggins, Newberry, South Carolina

FINNISH FISH SOUP

1 lb. fish fillets	4 med. potatoes, diced
1 tbsp. allspice	1 c. milk
2 tsp. salt	1 sm. can evaporated milk
1 med. onion, chopped	3 tbsp. butter

Cut the fish into 2-inch pieces. Place the fish, allspice, salt and onion in a saucepan, then add 4 cups water. Bring to a boil, then simmer until fish flakes easily when tested with a fork. Drain and reserve the stock. Place potatoes in a large saucepan and add the reserved stock, then cook until tender. Add the fish and milks and simmer for about 20 minutes. Pour into soup tureen and dot with butter. 6 servings.

Mrs. Becky Littleton, Macon, Georgia

FISH STEW

1/2 lb. salt pork, diced	1 tsp. cayenne pepper
2 lb. onions, diced	1/4 tsp. monosodium glutamate
2 cans tomato soup	Salt and pepper to taste
1 soup can water	1 tbsp. vinegar
1 14-oz. bottle catsup	3 lb. boned fish, flaked
Worcestershire sauce to taste	4 hard-boiled eggs, chopped

Fry the salt pork in a skillet until brown, then remove from drippings. Saute the onions in drippings until tender. Combine remaining ingredients except fish and eggs in a kettle and add the onions. Simmer for 30 minutes. Add the fish and simmer for 30 minutes longer. Add eggs and serve.

Mrs. W. B. McCurdy, Florence, South Carolina

FISH SOUP GRAVY

10 sm. pike fillets	2 bay leaves
3/4 c. vinegar	1 1/2 tsp. whole allspice
2 tbsp. butter	1 1/2 c. half and half
2 med. onions, sliced	6 tbsp. flour
2 tbsp. cocoa	Salt and pepper to taste

Soak the fillets in vinegar for several hours. Combine 6 cups water, butter, onions, cocoa, bay leaves and allspice in a large saucepan and bring to a boil. Cook for 15 minutes, then add the fillets and vinegar and cook for 10 minutes longer. Remove the fillets and strain the broth. Return the broth to the saucepan and bring to a boil. Combine the half and half and flour, and stir into the broth, then cook, stirring constantly, until thickened. Return the fillets and season with salt and pepper, then heat through. Serve over potatoes or bread.

Mrs. Amy Black, Dover, Delaware

FISH GUMBO

1 lb. frozen fish fillets	2 tsp. salt
1/3 c. butter	1/4 tsp. pepper
2 lge. onions, chopped	1 bay leaf
2 green peppers, chopped	1 c. cooked rice
2 No. 2 cans tomatoes and okra	

Thaw the fish fillets to room temperature. Melt the butter in a large saucepan, then add the onions and green peppers, and cook until tender. Stir in the tomatoes and okra, salt, pepper and bay leaf. Cook over low heat for at least 15 minutes. Cut the fish fillets into cubes, then add with the rice to the gumbo and

Fish Gumbo (above)

cook for about 8 minutes or until fish flakes easily when tested with a fork. 4 servings.

BAY COLONY GUMBO

3/4 c. flour	1 can tomatoes
1/3 c. bacon drippings	2 lb. peeled fresh shrimp
1 c. diced celery	1 pod hot pepper
1 c. diced onions	1 c. sliced okra
2 cloves of garlic	1 lb. white crab meat
1/2 c. diced green pepper	Salt and pepper to taste

Brown the flour slowly in bacon drippings in a Dutch oven, then add the celery, onions, garlic and green pepper. Cook until onions are soft. Add the tomatoes and 1 can water and simmer, stirring occasionally, for 1 hour. Add the shrimp, hot pepper and okra and simmer for 30 minutes longer, adding water if needed. Stir in the crab meat, salt and pepper. Serve over steamed rice.

Mrs. James Pizzotti, Fairhope, Alabama

FISH CHOWDER

2 lb. haddock	1 bay leaf, crumbled
1/2 c. diced salt pork	1 tsp. salt
2 onions, sliced	Pepper to taste
4 lge. potatoes, diced	1 qt. milk
1 c. chopped celery	2 tbsp. butter

Place the haddock and 2 cups water in a saucepan and bring to a boil. Simmer for 15 minutes, then drain and reserve broth. Remove haddock from bones and discard bones. Cook the salt pork in a skillet until crisp. Remove from skillet and set aside. Saute onions in pork fat until golden brown and place in a large saucepan. Add the haddock, potatoes, celery, bay leaf, salt and pepper. Add enough boiling water to reserved broth to make 3 cups liquid and pour into haddock mixture. Simmer for 30 minutes. Add milk and butter and simmer for 5 minutes longer. Sprinkle with salt pork.

Mrs. Wanda Kyles, Cleveland, North Carolina

MARYLAND SEAFOOD CHOWDER

1/2 lb. salt pork, diced	1/8 tsp. pepper
8 onions, cut into rings	1 tsp. paprika
8 med. potatoes, diced	2 qt. milk
2 lb. haddock fillet, cubed	1 1/2 c. evaporated milk
1 tsp. salt	

Fry the pork slowly in a large heavy kettle until lightly browned. Add the onions, potatoes, haddock and 4 cups water and cook for 15 minutes or until vegetables are tender. Add the seasonings and milks, then simmer until heated through. Cool for several hours, then heat through to serve.

Mrs. Grace Cummings, Baltimore, Maryland

MULLET STEW

1 2-lb. mullet	1 lge. onion, sliced
2 potatoes, thinly sliced	1/4 stick margarine
Salt and pepper to taste	

Remove mullet from bones and cut the mullet in small pieces. Place alternate layers of mullet, potatoes, salt, pepper, onion and margarine in a heavy saucepan and pour in 1 cup water. Cook over low heat until mullet is tender.

Nellie Batten, Whiteville, North Carolina

JIFFY LOBSTER STEW

2 5-oz. cans lobster	1 14-oz. can evaporated
1 can cream of mushroom	milk
soup	1 8-oz. bottle clam juice
1 can chicken and rice	3 tbsp. bourbon
soup	

Drain the lobster and place in the top of a 2-quart double boiler. Add the remaining ingredients and mix until blended. Place over hot water and simmer for 30 minutes. 3-4 servings.

Mrs. Irene Gilbert, Alexandria, Virginia

LOBSTER BISQUE

1 can cream of mushroom	1/8 tsp. paprika
soup	1 c. cooked lobster
1 can cream of celery soup	1 2-oz. can mushrooms,
1 1/2 c. milk	drained

Combine the soups, milk and paprika in a saucepan, then stir until well blended. Simmer until heated through, then add the lobster and mushrooms. Heat thoroughly before serving.

Mrs. Jessie Cook, Ozark, Alabama

LOBSTER GUMBO

3 tbsp. butter	1 No. 2 can tomatoes
1 onion, chopped	1/2 lb. okra, sliced
1 clove of garlic	1/2 bay leaf
1/2 c. chopped celery	Salt to taste
1 lb. cooked lobster,	1/2 tsp. pepper
diced	

Melt the butter in a deep kettle and saute the onion, garlic and celery for 10 minutes. Remove the garlic and add the lobster, tomatoes, okra, bay leaf, salt and pepper. Stir in 4 cups boiling water. Cover and bring to a boil slowly, then reduce the heat. Simmer for 40 minutes. Serve in bowls over hot rice.

Mamie Ellsberry, Birmingham, Alabama

LOBSTER STEW SUPREME

1 lb. lobster meat, chopped	4 c. milk
1 stick butter	Salt and pepper to taste
2 cans cream of mushroom soup	

Saute the lobster meat in the butter in a frypan over low heat until golden. Stir in the soup gradually. Scald the milk in a saucepan, then add the lobster mixture, salt and pepper. Refrigerate for several hours for flavors to blend, then heat thoroughiy before serving. 6 servings.

Mrs. Paula Dukes, Arlington, Virginia

ROCK LOBSTER-CORN SOUP STEW

2 8-oz. packages frozen South African rock lobster-tails	1/4 c. flour
	4 c. milk
1/4 c. butter or margarine	1 1-lb. can cream-style corn
1 sm. onion, minced	Salt to taste
1/2 c. chopped celery	Paprika to taste
1/2 c. chopped fresh mushrooms	Cayenne pepper to taste

Thaw the lobster-tails, then remove the underside membrane with scissors. Remove the meat in 1 piece and cut into crosswise slices. Melt the butter in a 3-quart saucepan, then add onion, celery and mushrooms and saute until tender but not brown. Stir in the flour, then add the milk slowly, stirring constantly. Cook over low heat, stirring constantly, until soup thickens slightly. Add the corn and lobster pieces. Season with the salt, paprika and cayenne pepper. Cook over low heat, stirring, until lobster is white and opaque. Sprinkle with paprika at serving time, if desired. 6-8 servings.

Rock Lobster-Corn Soup Stew (above)

65

BLENDER OYSTER STEW

1 8-oz. can oysters	2 c. milk
1 c. water	1/4 tsp. salt
3 tbsp. margarine	1 tsp. chili powder

Place the oysters and water in a blender container and chop for 2 seconds. Pour in a saucepan and simmer for 2 to 3 minutes, stirring occasionally. Add the margarine, milk and salt and heat through. Do not boil. Stir in the chili powder just before serving. 4-6 servings.

Mrs. Roy Harwood, Taylor, Texas

OYSTER CHOWDER

2 lge. potatoes, diced	2 cans oysters
1/2 lb. bacon, diced	3 c. warm milk
2 lge. onions, diced	Salt and pepper to taste
2 tbsp. flour	

Cook the potatoes in a small amount of water until tender. Fry the bacon until crisp, then add the onions and cook until limp. Drain off the excess fat, then stir in the flour. Add the oysters and juice, then stir in the milk. Add the potatoes, salt and pepper and simmer until heated through. Serve with crackers. 8 servings.

Mrs. Franklin Oates, Lepanto, Arkansas

STRETCHER OYSTER STEW

1 pt. oysters	1 c. light cream
Milk	1/8 tsp. pepper
2 c. diced potatoes	1/4 tsp. paprika
1/3 c. butter	

Drain the oysters and reserve the liquor, then chop the oysters coarsely. Add enough milk to the reserved oyster liquor to make 2 cups liquid. Cook the potatoes in a large saucepan in a small amount of salted water until almost tender. Add the oysters and milk mixture, then bring to a boil. Remove from heat and add the butter, cream, pepper and paprika. Cover and let stand for 15 minutes. Heat through before serving. 5-6 servings.

Mrs. Elsie Lansing, Norfolk, Virginia

OYSTER BISQUE

1 12-oz. can fresh oysters	1 tsp. garlic salt
3 c. milk	2 tsp. Worcestershire sauce
1 bay leaf	Dash of nutmeg

2 tbsp. butter
1/4 c. instant mashed
   potato granules

1 egg, separated
1 tomato soup

Drop the oysters into boiling water and cook for 5 minutes. Drain and chop. Combine the milk, seasonings and butter in a saucepan, then bring almost to a boil. Stir in the potato granules. Stir a small amount of the milk mixture into the slightly beaten egg yolk, then return to the milk mixture, stirring until blended. Add the soup and mix well. Add the oysters and simmer for 5 minutes. Beat the egg white until stiff peaks form, then fold into the oyster mixture. Garnish with parsley and serve immediately.

Mrs. Joyce Blackwell, Austin, Texas

HOLIDAY OYSTER STEW

2 12-oz. cans fresh oysters
2 slices bacon, chopped
1/3 c. chopped onion
Half and half

1 can frozen cream of potato
  soup
1 1/4 tsp. salt
Dash of white pepper

Drain the oysters and reserve the liquor. Fry the bacon until crisp, then remove the bacon from the fat. Cook the onion in the bacon fat until tender. Add enough half and half to the reserved oyster liquor to make 4 cups liquid. Combine all the ingredients except the bacon and oysters, then cook until heated through. Add the oysters and cook for 3 to 5 minutes longer or until edges of oysters begin to curl. Sprinkle the bacon over the top. Garnish with chopped parsley, pimento stars and oyster crackers just before serving.

Holiday Oyster Stew (above)

SALMON BISQUE

1 1-lb. can pink salmon	4 tbsp. flour
1 c. canned tomatoes	3 c. milk
1/2 c. chopped onion	1 1/2 tsp. salt
2 tbsp. chopped parsley	1/2 tsp. paprika
4 tbsp. butter	

Combine the salmon, tomatoes, onion, parsley and 2 cups water in a saucepan and simmer for 20 minutes. Melt the butter in a large saucepan and blend in flour, then stir in the milk slowly. Add the salt and paprika and cook, stirring constantly, until thickened and smooth. Stir in the salmon mixture slowly and heat thoroughly. Do not boil. 5 servings.

Mrs. Theresa Comer, Lexington, Kentucky

SALMON-POTATO SOUP

4 med. potatoes, diced	1 sm. onion, minced
1 qt. milk	Salt and pepper to taste
1 pt. half and half	1 No. 2 can salmon,
1 stick butter	flaked

Cook the potatoes in salted water to cover in a large saucepan until just tender. Add the remaining ingredients and simmer for 20 minutes. 4-6 servings.

Mrs. Anna Marie Holmes, Murfreesboro, Tennessee

SOUP ALASKA

1 1-lb. can pink salmon	1 tsp. salt
1 qt. milk	1/8 tsp. pepper
1 6-oz. can evaporated milk	

Remove bones and skin from salmon, but do not drain. Combine the salmon, milks, salt and pepper in top of a double boiler. Place over boiling water and cook until heated through. Garnish with paprika or parsley flakes. Two 6 1/2-ounce cans tuna may be substituted for salmon.

Mrs. Irving W. Hazard, DeLand, Florida

BOUILLABAISSE

1/4 c. oil	1 c. stewed tomatoes
1 carrot, diced	1 bay leaf
2 onions, chopped	1/2 tsp. thyme
1 celery stalk and top, diced	1/8 tsp. saffron
1 leek, chopped	2 tbsp. soy flour
1/4 c. chopped fennel	2 c. fish stock or water
1 clove of garlic, minced	1 tsp. salt

1 tsp. minced dulse	2 tbsp. lemon juice
1 doz. scallops	1 c. apple cider

Heat the oil in a large pot, then add the carrot, onions, celery, leek, fennel and garlic and saute lightly. Stir in the tomatoes, bay leaf, thyme, saffron, flour, stock, salt and dulse. Cover and simmer for 20 minutes. Remove the bay leaf, then add the scallops, lemon juice and cider and cook for 10 minutes longer. Serve with French bread. 6-8 servings.

Mrs. Alice Taylor, Palm Beach, Florida

SOUTH FRANCE FISH SOUP

1 lb. mackerel fillets	1 bay leaf
1/2 lb. halibut fillets	Grated rind of 1/4 lemon
1 lb. flounder fillets	1 1/2 tsp. salt
4 med. tomatoes	Freshly ground pepper to taste
4 med. potatoes	2 tbsp. white wine
3 cloves of garlic	2 tsp. chili powder
1 leek, sliced	5 thick slices homemade bread
2 sprigs of parsley	1 tbsp. olive oil

Cut the fish fillets in large pieces. Scald the tomatoes and remove the skins, then cut into wedges. Peel and slice the potatoes. Place the fish, tomatoes and potatoes in a soup kettle. Crush 1 clove of garlic and add to the fish mixture, then add the leek, parsley, bay leaf and lemon rind. Pour in 6 cups boiling water, then add the salt, pepper and wine. Bring to a boil and cook for 20 minutes or until the fish and potatoes test done. Crush the remaining garlic and stir in the chili powder. Remove the crust from 1 slice of bread and soak in a small amount of water. Squeeze out and combine with the garlic mixture. Stir in the oil and 3 or 4 tablespoons of the fish stock. Spread on the remaining bread slices and place in soup bowls. Spoon the fish and potatoes over the bread. 4 servings.

South France Fish Soup (above)

SHRIMP STEW

1 lge. onion, chopped	1 lge. can stewed tomatoes
2 stalks celery, chopped	1 can tomato paste
1 tbsp. minced green pepper	Salt and pepper to taste
2 tsp. chopped parsley	2 lb. shelled shrimp,
1 clove of garlic, chopped	deveined
2 tbsp. cooking oil	

Saute the onion, celery, green pepper, parsley and garlic in the oil until lightly browned in a large saucepan. Add the remaining ingredients except the shrimp and simmer for 1 hour, adding water if needed. Add the shrimp and cook for 15 minutes longer. Serve in soup bowls over rice. 8-10 servings.

Mrs. Florence Chambless, Eros, Louisiana

TUNA CHOWDER

1 med. potato, diced	1/4 c. butter or margarine
2 c. stewed tomatoes	1/4 c. all-purpose flour
1 med. onion, chopped	3 c. milk
1/2 tsp. celery seed	2 tsp. salt
2 c. water	1/4 tsp. pepper
2 6 1/2-oz. cans solid-pack tuna	Finely chopped parsley

Combine the potato, tomatoes, onion, celery seed and water in a 4-quart saucepan, then bring to a boil. Reduce the heat to low and simmer for 30 minutes, stirring occasionally. Drain the tuna and break into chunks, then add to the potato mixture. Melt the butter over low heat, then stir in the flour until well blended. Add the milk gradually and cook until thickened, stirring constantly. Add the salt and pepper. Stir into the tuna mixture and mix well. Sprinkle with parsley and serve hot. 6 servings.

Mrs. E. S. Davenport, West Columbia, South Carolina

POTATO-TUNA SOUP

1 tbsp. chopped onion	1 tsp. salt
2 qt. milk	1/4 tsp. pepper
1 6 1/2-oz. can tuna	1/2 tsp. paprika
6 c. diced cooked potatoes	1 tbsp. butter
1 tsp. celery salt	

Cook the onion in 1 cup milk for 5 minutes. Place the remaining milk in a large saucepan, then add the onion mixture and the remaining ingredients. Simmer for 20 minutes. Turn into soup tureen and garnish with chopped parsley. 10-12 servings.

Mrs. Susan Hartley, Westminster, Maryland

TURTLE SOUP

1 1/2 c. diced turtle meat	3 drops of hot sauce
2 qt. beef stock	1 hard-cooked egg white,
1 bay leaf	diced
1/2 tsp. mace	Salt and pepper to taste
1 1/2 tbsp. lemon juice	1/4 c. sherry

Combine the turtle meat, beef stock, bay leaf, mace, lemon juice and hot sauce in a large saucepan, then bring to a boil and cook until the turtle meat is tender. Remove the bay leaf and add the egg white. Season with salt and pepper, then add the sherry just before serving. 8 servings.

Mrs. Nancy Ames, Silver Spring, Maryland

SPINACH SOUP WITH FISH

1 pkg. frozen fish fillets	Dash of pepper
2 pkg. frozen chopped spinach	1 nutmeg, grated
4 c. chicken bouillon	2 tbsp. butter
1 1/2 tsp. salt	3 slices bread, cubed

Thaw the fish, then cut into bite-sized pieces. Cook the spinach according to package directions in a large saucepan, then add the bouillon, salt, pepper, nutmeg and fish. Cook until the fish flakes easily. Melt the butter in a skillet, then add the bread and fry, stirring frequently, until brown and crisp. Serve the soup in bowls and sprinkle the bread cubes over the top.

Spinach Soup with Fish (above)

Baked Gefilte Fish (page 74)

baked seafood

A convenient dry heat method of cooking seafood is baking. In this chapter devoted entirely to baked seafood, you will find a delightful variety of recipes, many of which contain sauces or stuffings. These added ingredients not only impart a special flavor to the baking fish or shellfish but also keep it moist and tender.

Adding sauces to baking seafood is one way of assuring flavorful and succulent baked dishes. Wine and sherry make delicately light sauces that complement the flavor of seafood exceptionally well. For example, in Sherried Flounder the fish is accented with a mixture of sherry, mushrooms, and curry powder. For a richer, zestier sauce, turn to Grouper Parmesan, a baked dish that combines sour cream, parmesan cheese, and a dash of hot pepper sauce.

Seafood stuffings provide the fish or shellfish with a flavorful source of internal moisture during cooking. They usually consist of bread or cracker crumbs, or corn meal and a variety of finely chopped vegetables. Particularly well suited to stuffing are whole fish or fillets. Of the many outstanding recipes for stuffed fish, you will certainly be delighted with Baked Stuffed Red Snapper and Whitefish with Dill Cheese Stuffing.

Baking is a genuinely effortless way to prepare moist and tender seafood, especially with the assortment of recipes contained in this chapter.

BAKED GEFILTE FISH

1 lb. whitefish fillets	1/4 tsp. pepper
1 lb. halibut fillets	1 egg, beaten
1/2 c. fine dry bread crumbs	2 8-oz. cans tomato sauce
1 tsp. salt	2 tbsp. peanut oil
1/2 tsp. onion powder	1 tsp. seasoned salt

Grind the whitefish and halibut fillets together, then combine with the bread crumbs, salt, onion powder and 1/8 teaspoon pepper. Add the egg and mix thoroughly. Shape into 8 balls. Place in a casserole. Combine the tomato sauce, oil, seasoned salt and remaining pepper. Pour over the fish balls. Bake, covered, in a 375 degree oven for 45 minutes or until done. Garnish with sprigs of parsley to serve. 8 servings.

Photograph for this recipe on page 72.

CORN CRISP CATFISH

1/2 c. evaporated milk	1/4 tsp. pepper
1 c. corn flake crumbs	1 1/2 lb. blue catfish
1 tsp. monosodium glutamate	steaks
1 tsp. salt	

Pour the milk in a bowl. Combine the corn flake crumbs, monosodium glutamate, salt and pepper in another bowl. Dip the steaks in the milk, then roll in the crumb mixture. Arrange in a shallow pan. Bake in 375-degree oven for about 20 minutes or until done.

Mrs. Paul Richardson, Hawesville, Kentucky

CRAB MEAT AND SHRIMP AU GRATIN

1 c. minced onion	1 tsp. salt
1 stalk celery, chopped fine	1/2 tsp. red pepper
1/2 stick margarine	1/4 tsp. pepper
2 tbsp. flour	3 tbsp. sherry
1 13-oz. can evaporated milk	1 lb. white crab meat
milk	1 lb. cooked shrimp
2 egg yolks, beaten	1/2 lb. grated Cheddar cheese

Saute the onion and celery in the margarine until wilted, then blend in the flour. Combine the milk and eggs, then add gradually to flour mixture, stirring constantly. Add the salt, peppers and sherry and cook, stirring constantly, for 5 minutes. Combine the crab meat and shrimp in a bowl, then pour in the sherry sauce, mixing well. Turn into a greased baking dish and sprinkle with the cheese. Bake at 375 degrees for 15 minutes or until the cheese is melted.

Mrs. John L. Black, Jr., Jackson, Mississippi

SEAFOOD IN WINE SAUCE

1 stick butter	1/8 c. chopped parsley
1/2 c. flour	1/2 c. dry white wine
4 c. milk	1/2 lb. sauteed mushrooms
Salt and pepper to taste	1 lb. cooked cleaned shrimp
1/4 tsp. paprika	2 c. lobster meat
1/4 c. chopped chives	1 c. crab meat

Melt the butter in a saucepan, then blend in the flour. Add the milk gradually and cook, stirring constantly, until thick and smooth. Season with the salt, pepper, paprika, chives and parsley. Add the wine and mushrooms and mix gently. Place the shrimp, lobster and crab meat in a 2-quart baking dish and cover with the sauce. Bake at 350 degrees for 20 minutes, then broil for 1 minute. Serve immediately.

Mrs. W. C. Stinson, Greenwood, Mississippi

BAKED MUSSEL OMELET

1 c. thick white sauce	5 eggs
1 c. mussels, drained	2 tbsp. margarine
Salt	3 tbsp. grated cheese
Pepper to taste	

Combine the white sauce and mussels in a saucepan, then season with salt and pepper. Simmer until heated through. Combine the eggs, 2 tablespoons water and 1 teaspoon salt in a bowl and beat well. Melt the margarine in an omelet pan, then pour in the egg mixture. Cook until bottom is lightly browned and center is just set, then roll up and place on a ovenproof serving dish. Sprinkle the cheese over the top, then pour the sauce over the cheese. Bake at 350 degrees until cheese is melted and sauce is bubbly. Serve immediately.

Baked Mussel Omelet (above)

CRAB MEAT PIE

1 unbaked 8-in. pastry shell	1/4 c. chopped green pepper
1 7 1/2-oz. can crab meat	1 c. mayonnaise
1 c. chopped celery	1 tbsp. lemon juice
Dash of salt	3/4 c. toasted bread crumbs
1 tbsp. grated onion	Shredded cheese

Prick the bottom and side of the pastry shell. Bake at 400 degrees for 10 to 12 minutes or until lightly browned, then set aside. Combine the crab meat, celery, salt, onion, green pepper, mayonnaise, lemon juice and 1/2 cup bread crumbs, tossing to mix well, then turn into the pie shell. Sprinkle with remaining bread crumbs and cheese. Bake at 400 degrees for 10 minutes or until cheese melts. 4-6 servings.

Mrs. Byard Edwards, Shelby, North Carolina

HOT CRAB MEAT PIE

1 7 1/2-oz. can Alaska King crab	2 tbsp. instant minced onion
	1/2 tsp. horseradish
2 3-oz. packages cream cheese	1/4 tsp. salt
	1/3 c. sliced almonds
1 tbsp. milk	Paprika

Drain the crab meat and flake. Soften the cream cheese at room temperature and blend with the milk until smooth. Add the onion, horseradish, salt and almonds, then mix in the crab meat. Spoon into an 8-inch pie plate or 4 individual dishes and sprinkle with paprika. Bake at 375 degrees for 15 to 20 minutes or until brown.

Mrs. Charles R. Haile, Jackson, Tennessee

INDIVIDUAL CRAB CASSOLETTES

3 tbsp. butter	1/2 tsp. salt
3 tbsp. flour	Pepper to taste
2 c. milk	1/4 tsp. dry mustard
2 eggs, beaten	1 c. Alaska King crab meat
2/3 c. grated Cheddar cheese	

Melt the butter in a saucepan and blend in the flour. Add the milk and cook, stirring constantly, over medium heat until the mixture thickens. Combine the eggs, cheese, salt, pepper, mustard and crab meat and blend well, then stir into the milk mixture and heat through. Place in 4 small or 2 medium custard cups. Bake at 375 degrees for 25 minutes or until brown and bubbly.

Mrs. D. V. Merrifield, Huntsville, Alabama

BASS FEREZANA

1/4 c. pignolias	1/2 c. raisins
1/4 c. butter or margarine	1/2 med. green pepper, chopped
1/2 c. thinly sliced leek	1 c. chopped cooked shrimp
1/4 lb. mushrooms, chopped	1/2 c. small pimento-stuffed olives
2 med. carrots, grated	

Salt and pepper to taste
1 3 to 4-lb. striped bass,
   cleaned

3 tbsp. butter, melted
3 tbsp. olive oil
1/2 c. brandy

Saute the pignolias in a saucepan in 1/4 cup butter until lightly brown. Remove the pignolias with a slotted spoon and set aside. Add the leek and mushrooms to the pan and saute until tender but not browned. Add the carrots, raisins and green pepper, then cover and cook over low heat for 5 minutes. Stir in the shrimp and olives and season with the salt and pepper, then set aside. Place the bass in a large shallow roasting dish. Pour the melted butter, oil and 1/4 cup of the brandy over the bass, then sprinkle with salt and pepper. Bake, uncovered, in a 400-degree oven for 15 minutes. Spoon the olive mixture around the bass, then sprinkle with the pignolias. Heat the remaining brandy, then ignite and pour over the olive mixture and bass. Bake for 15 to 20 minutes longer or until the fish flakes easily with a fork, basting occasionally with the pan drippings. Serve with parslied potatoes.

Photograph for this recipe on page 2.

FLOUNDER ROLLS

1 pkg. frozen flounder fillets
Salt to taste
1 1/2 tbsp. minced dillweed
1 1/2 tbsp. minced parsley

1 1/2 tbsp. minced chives
1/4 c. margarine
Fine dry bread crumbs
5/8 c. cream

Thaw the fillets, then rub with salt. Combine the dillweed, parsley and chives with the 2 tablespoons margarine, then spread over the fillets. Roll up the fillets and place in a greased baking dish. Sift the bread crumbs over the fillets, then drizzle the remaining melted margarine over top. Broil for about 10 minutes or until lightly browned. Add the cream to the baking dish and broil until browned and fish flakes easily.

Flounder Rolls (above)

SHERRIED FLOUNDER

1 lb. flounder fillets	Dash of salt
1/3 c. minced onion	Pepper to taste
1/2 c. sherry	Paprika to taste
1 4-oz. can chopped mushrooms	1/2 tsp. curry powder

Arrange the flounder in a buttered shallow baking dish and sprinkle with the onion. Add the sherry, mushrooms with liquid and seasonings. Bake, uncovered, at 350 degrees for about 30 minutes or until the flounder flakes easily when tested with fork.

Mrs. Rudolph Howell, Valdosta, Georgia

BAKED FLOUNDER

3 slices bacon	6 med. potatoes
1 3-lb. flounder, dressed	1 sm. onion, thinly sliced
Salt	3 ripe tomatoes, sliced
Cornmeal	

Cut each bacon slice in about 4 pieces. Cut slashes across the flounder about 1 inch apart and sprinkle with 1 teaspoon salt. Sprinkle a small amount of sifted cornmeal over the flounder and place the bacon in the slashes. Place the flounder in a greased pan. Bake at 350 degrees for 10 minutes. Wash, peel and slice the potatoes. Remove the flounder from the oven and place the potatoes over and around the flounder. Place the onion over the potatoes and sprinkle with salt. Cover and return to the oven. Bake for 20 to 30 minutes or until the potatoes are tender. Place the tomatoes on top. Reduce the temperature to 325 degrees and bake for 30 minutes longer.

Mrs. C. W. Prescott, Jacksonville, North Carolina

SALMON-CHEESE PIE

1 lge. can red salmon	Salt to taste
1/4 c. slivered onion	1 can refrigerator biscuits
1 can cheese soup	Parsley flakes
1 can green peas, drained	

Spread the salmon evenly in a buttered 2-quart baking dish. Sprinkle the onion over the salmon. Layer the soup and peas over the onion and sprinkle with salt. Top with a layer of biscuits. Sprinkle with parsley flakes. Bake at 400 degrees until the biscuits are golden brown. 6 servings.

Mrs. Patricia Wadkins, Little Rock, Arkansas

SALMON LOAF

1 1-lb. can salmon	2 eggs, beaten
1/2 c. cracker crumbs	1 sm. onion, minced

2 stalks celery, minced	Salt to taste
1/4 tsp. pepper	1/2 can cream of chicken
4 tbsp. mayonnaise	soup
1 c. cooked rice	

Drain the salmon, reserving the juice, then remove the skin and bones. Combine the salmon and reserved juice with the crumbs in a bowl, then add the eggs, onion, celery, pepper, mayonnaise, rice, salt and soup. Mix well and place in a greased loaf pan. Bake at 350 degrees for 45 minutes. Serve with Olive Sauce.

Olive Sauce

1/2 c. milk	12 sliced stuffed olives
2 tbsp. mayonnaise	1/2 can cream of celery
1 tsp. olive juice	soup

Combine the milk, mayonnaise, olive juice, olives and soup in a saucepan. Cook, stirring, over boiling water over low heat until blended and heated through.

Mrs. G. V. King, Hendersonville, North Carolina

BREEZY SALMON BAKE

2 lb. salmon steaks	Dash of pepper
2 tbsp. grated onion	1 tbsp. butter
1 1/4 tsp. dillweed	3/4 c. light cream
1 tsp. salt	

Place the steaks in a single layer in a well-greased 12 x 8 x 2-inch baking dish. Sprinkle with onion, dillweed, salt and pepper, then dot with butter. Pour the cream over the steaks. Bake at 350 degrees for 25 to 30 minutes or until steaks flake easily when tested with a fork. 6 servings.

Breezy Salmon Bake (above)

Deviled South African Rock Lobster (below)

DEVILED SOUTH AFRICAN ROCK LOBSTER

6 8-oz. South African rock lobster-tails	1 tsp. dry mustard
1 1/2 c. soft bread crumbs	1/2 tsp. salt
1 c. milk	Dash of cayenne pepper
1 egg, well beaten	1/2 c. soda cracker crumbs
	1/4 c. melted butter

Preheat the oven to 375 degrees. Drop the lobster-tails into boiling salted water. Bring to a boil and cook for 2 minutes. Drain immediately and rinse with cold water. Cut away the underside membrane and remove the meat, reserving the shells. Dice the lobster meat and mix with the bread crumbs, milk, egg, mustard, salt and cayenne pepper. Spoon the mixture into the reserved shells, then place in a shallow baking pan. Mix the cracker crumbs and butter and sprinkle over the top of the filled shells. Bake for 30 minutes or until crumbs are well browned. 6 servings.

SALMON SOUFFLE

3 tbsp. butter	1/2 tsp. salt
3 tbsp. flour	1/4 tsp. pepper
1 c. milk	1 lge. can pink salmon
1/2 onion, finely minced	3 eggs, separated

Melt the butter, then blend in the flour. Add the milk, onion and seasonings and cook, stirring, until smooth and thickened. Flake the salmon and beat the egg yolks, then add to the white sauce. Beat the egg whites until stiff and fold into the salmon mixture. Pour into a baking dish. Bake in 325-degree oven for 40 minutes or until firm.

Mrs. Mary Lee Sheets, Knoxville, Tennessee

SALMON TIMBALES

1 1-lb. can red salmon	1 tbsp. grated onion
1 c. bread crumbs	2 eggs, beaten
1/4 c. milk	1 tsp. lemon juice
2 tbsp. butter	Salt and pepper to taste

Remove bones from the salmon. Combine the salmon and liquid, bread crumbs and remaining ingredients and mix well. Place in greased custard cups. Bake at 350 degrees for 30 minutes. Unmold and serve with cheese sauce, if desired.

Mrs. William N. Orr, Littlefield, Texas

SALMON WITH WATER CHESTNUT DRESSING

8 salmon steaks, 1/4-in. thick	1 5-oz. can water chestnuts
1 1/4 c. white wine	1 pkg. frozen spinach
2 eggs, slightly beaten	1 8-oz. package herb-seasoned stuffing mix
1 can cream of chicken soup	2 tbsp. butter, melted

Marinate the salmon in 1/2 cup wine for 30 minutes. Combine the eggs, soup and remaining wine, beating until smooth. Drain and slice the water chestnuts and thaw the spinach. Add the water chestnuts, spinach, stuffing mix and butter to the soup mixture. Arrange the salmon in a foil-lined shallow pan and top with the dressing, patting down firmly. Bake at 350 degrees for 45 minutes or until the dressing is brown. 8 servings.

Mrs. Margaret Flint, Tucson, Arizona

BAKED HALIBUT IN SOUR CREAM

6 halibut steaks	1/8 c. chopped pimento
1 pt. sour cream	1/2 tsp. dry mustard
1/4 c. chopped onion	1/2 tsp. dry basil
1/4 c. chopped dill pickles	1/8 c. lemon juice
1/8 c. chopped parsley	Grated Parmesan cheese

Place the halibut in a buttered baking pan. Mix the remaining ingredients except the cheese and spread over the halibut. Sprinkle the cheese on top. Bake at 375 degrees for 25 to 30 minutes or until fish flakes easily. 6 servings.

Mrs. Doris Prater, Jackson, Mississippi

BAKED STUFFED HALIBUT

1 3-lb. halibut	1 sm. onion, chopped
2 firm tomatoes, chopped	2 stalks of celery, chopped
1/2 c. chopped green pepper	Salt and pepper to taste

Cut the halibut almost in half. Combine the chopped vegetables and stuff into the halibut. Sprinkle with salt and pepper. Close with toothpicks or skewers and place in an oiled shallow pan. Bake for 30 minutes in a 350-degree oven. 2 servings.

Mrs. Dianne Pruett, Baltimore, Maryland

HALIBUT WITH VEGETABLES

4 carrots	2 tsp. salt
4 slices bacon	Pepper
1 lge. onion	2 lb. halibut fillets
1/4 lb. mushrooms	4 slices lemon
2 tbsp. chopped parsley	1/4 c. butter
3 tbsp. minced celery	1 c. dry white wine
1 tsp. chopped dill	

Wash the carrots and slice thin. Place the bacon slices in a shallow baking dish and spread with the carrots. Chop the onion and mushrooms and spread over the carrots. Sprinkle with the parsley, celery, dill, 1 teaspoon salt and a small amount of pepper. Place the halibut on top and sprinkle with the remaining salt. Place the lemon slices over the halibut, then dot with butter and pour the wine over all. Cover tightly with foil. Bake in a 400-degree oven for 20 minutes. Remove the foil and bake for 20 minutes longer.

Mrs. Nimie Anderson, Jacksonville, Florida

MEXICAN-STYLE BAKED OYSTERS

1/2 c. tomato catsup	1 qt. large oysters
1 tsp. Worcestershire sauce	1/2 c. grated American cheese
1/2 tsp. salt	1 tbsp. butter
Dash of pepper	Sliced dill pickles

Combine the catsup, Worcestershire sauce, salt and pepper. Place the oysters in a buttered baking dish and cover with the catsup mixture. Sprinkle with grated cheese and dot with butter. Bake in 350-degree oven until the cheese is melted and the oysters are curled. Serve hot and garnish with dill pickle slices.

Mrs. W. P. Vaughan, Katy, Texas

BAKED OYSTERS

1 lge. onion, finely chopped	1 c. chopped celery
1/2 c. finely chopped parsley	2 tbsp. cooking oil

50 oysters, well drained	10 saltine crackers, crushed
1 egg, well beaten	Butter

Saute the onion, parsley and celery in hot oil in a skillet until tender. Add the oysters and stir once. Remove from heat and add the egg. Return to the heat and cook, stirring, until the egg is done. Add the cracker crumbs and stir well. Place on oyster half shells or in a shallow baking dish and dot with butter. Bake in 400-degree oven for several minutes or until brown.

Mrs. C. W. Adams, Mobile, Alabama

OVEN-FRIED OYSTERS

1 c. flour	1 egg, slightly beaten
1 tsp. salt	Bread crumbs
1/4 tsp. pepper	Salad oil
1 doz. oysters	

Combine the flour, salt and pepper. Roll the oysters in the seasoned flour then dip in the egg. Coat the oysters in bread crumbs, then dip in the oil. Place in a shallow pan. Bake at 400 degrees for 30 minutes or until brown. 2 servings.

Mrs. Elizabeth Powell, Baltimore, Maryland

OYSTER-MUSHROOM BAKE

2 tbsp. butter	1/2 c. chopped mushrooms
2 tbsp. finely chopped	Salt and pepper to taste
onion	20 med. oysters
2 tbsp. chopped parsley	Bread or cracker crumbs

Melt the butter in a skillet, then add the onion, parsley, mushrooms, salt and pepper. Saute over low heat for 5 minutes or until the onion is soft. Place the oysters in a single layer in a buttered baking dish. Pour the mushroom mixture over the oysters. Top with bread crumbs. Bake at 450 degrees for about 10 minutes or until the crumbs are brown. Serve hot. 4 servings.

Mrs. Robert Hogin, Tallahassee, Florida

OYSTER RAMEKINS

3 tbsp. butter	Salt and pepper to taste
2 tbsp. flour	Worcestershire sauce to
1 tbsp. minced green onion	taste
3 doz. oysters, drained	Cracker crumbs

Melt the butter in a skillet, then add the flour and cook, stirring constantly, until brown. Add the onion and oysters. Cook over low heat until the oysters begin to curl, then season with the salt, pepper and Worcestershire sauce. Place in ramekins or large shells and cover with crumbs. Bake in 350-degree oven until browned. 4 servings.

Tita O'Neill Stafford, Alexandria, Louisiana

Fish Baked with Clam Stuffing (below)

FISH BAKED WITH CLAM STUFFING

1 3 to 4-lb. fish	1 7-oz. can minced clams
Salt and pepper to taste	1/2 c. butter
1 pkg. herb-seasoned stuffing mix	Tomato, onion and lemon slices

Sprinkle the fish inside and out with salt and pepper. Combine the stuffing mix with the undrained clams and 1/4 cup melted butter. Arrange the fish and stuffing in a buttered baking dish. Dot the fish and stuffing with the remaining butter. Bake at 350 degrees for 30 to 40 minutes or until fish flakes easily when tested with a fork. Garnish with tomato, onion and lemon slices.

GROUPER PARMESAN

2 lb. grouper fillets	1 tbsp. grated onion
1 c. sour cream	1/2 tsp. salt
1/4 c. grated Parmesan cheese	Dash of hot sauce
1 tbsp. lemon juice	Paprika
	Chopped parsley

Thaw the grouper, if frozen. Skin the fillets and cut into serving portions. Place in a single layer in a well-greased 12 x 8 x 2-inch baking dish. Combine the remaining ingredients except the paprika and parsley. Spread the sour cream mixture over the grouper and sprinkle with paprika. Bake in a 350-degree oven for 25 to 30 minutes or until tender. Garnish with parsley.

Mrs. G. C. Booker, Warrington, Florida

QUICK-BAKED FISH

2 lb. fish fillets	2 tsp. salt
1/4 c. evaporated milk	2 c. fine, dry bread crumbs
1/4 c. water	2 tbsp. salad oil

Cut the fish fillets into serving portions. Combine the evaporated milk, water and salt. Dip the fish fillets in the milk mixture, then into bread crumbs until thickly coated. Place on an oiled shallow baking pan and drizzle each piece lightly with oil. Bake, uncovered, in 400-degree oven for 25 minutes. Do not turn fish or add water. Garnish with parsley or lemon. 5 servings.

Mrs. Glen S. Eckard, Goldsboro, North Carolina

BAKED HADDOCK

1 tsp. butter	3/4 c. grated sharp cheese
2 lb. haddock fillets	Paprika
2 cans cream of shrimp soup	

Grease a baking dish with the butter. Place the haddock in the dish and spread the thawed soup over the haddock. Sprinkle cheese and paprika over the soup. Bake for 1 hour at 375 degrees. 6 servings.

Alison Nolan, Natchez, Mississippi

BAKED HADDOCK WITH CELERY DRESSING

2 lb. fillets of haddock	1/3 c. chopped parsley
Salt and pepper to taste	1 c. soft bread crumbs
2 tbsp. lemon juice	1/2 tsp. sage
1/2 c. chopped celery	1/4 c. dry bread crumbs
1/3 c. chopped onion	Paprika
3 tbsp. butter	

Arrange half the fillets in a greased shallow pan and sprinkle with salt, pepper and lemon juice. Mix the celery, onion and butter together in a saucepan, then heat to melt the butter. Remove from heat and add the parsley, crumbs and sage. Toss to mix well. Add just enough hot water to moisten slightly. Spread the dressing over the fillets, and cover with the remaining fillets. Sprinkle the top with salt, pepper, dry bread crumbs and paprika. Pour 1/4 cup hot water into the baking dish. Bake at 375 degrees for 25 to 30 minutes. Serve hot. 6 servings.

Mrs. R. J. Barnes, Mine Run, Virginia

HADDOCK-SHRIMP BAKE

1 can frozen cream of shrimp soup	1/2 tsp. Worcestershire sauce
1 1-lb. package frozen haddock	1/4 tsp. garlic salt
fillets	1 1/4 c. crushed round buttery
1/4 lb. margarine	crackers
1/2 tsp. grated onion	

Thaw the soup. Thaw fillets slightly and place in a greased, shallow baking dish. Spread with soup. Bake in 375-degree oven for 20 minutes. Combine remaining ingredients and sprinkle over fish. Bake for 15 minutes longer.

Mrs. Marva Eaves, Waynesboro, Virginia

BAKED SCALLOPS

1/2 c. fine bread crumbs	1/4 tsp. pepper
1 onion, chopped	Butter
1/2 tsp. salt	1 lb. scallops

Place half the bread crumbs and onion in a baking dish and sprinkle with salt and pepper. Dot with butter. Place the scallops on the bread crumb mixture and cover with remaining crumbs, onion and seasoning. Dot with butter. Bake at 400 degrees for 25 to 30 minutes. 3 servings.

Frances McBride, Savannah, Georgia

SCALLOPS AU GRATIN

2 tbsp. butter	2 tbsp. chopped chives
2 tbsp. flour	1 lb. scallops
1 c. milk	1/2 c. buttered crumbs
1/4 tsp. salt	2 tbsp. grated cheese
1/4 tsp. pepper	

Melt the butter in a saucepan, then stir in the flour. Stir in the milk gradually and cook over low heat, stirring constantly, until thickened. Add the salt, pepper and chives. Add the scallops and simmer for 5 minutes. Pour into a buttered 2 1/2-quart baking dish. Top with the buttered crumbs and grated cheese. Bake for 30 minutes at 350 degrees or until brown and bubbly. 4 servings.

Mrs. Carolyn Garland, Wilmington, North Carolina

SCALLOPS IN WINE-CHEESE SAUCE

1 1/2 lb. scallops, chopped	3 tbsp. butter
1/2 c. dry white wine	3 tbsp. flour
1/2 tsp. salt	1/2 c. heavy cream
Dash of cayenne pepper	1 c. grated Cheddar cheese
1 tsp. instant minced onion	1/2 c. buttered crumbs

Combine the scallops with the wine, salt, cayenne pepper and onion in a saucepan and bring to a boil. Cover and simmer for 10 minutes. Drain, reserving 1 cup stock. Melt the butter and blend in the flour. Add the reserved stock and cream. Cook, stirring, until thickened. Stir in the cheese and scallops. Place in 6 large shells or individual baking dishes and top with crumbs. Bake at 400 degrees for 10 minutes. 6 servings.

Annabelle Gordon, Dover, Delaware

SAVORY SHRIMP

4 cloves of garlic	3 lb. small shrimp
1 c. butter	1 can consomme
2 c. dry bread crumbs	Salt and pepper to taste
6 tbsp. minced parsley	

Saute the garlic in butter for 10 minutes, then remove and discard the garlic. Add the crumbs and parsley to the butter. Shell and devein the shrimp and place in a shallow baking dish. Cover with consomme. Season with salt and pepper. Sprinkle the crumb mixture over the shrimp. Bake at 400 degrees for 15 minutes or until brown. 6 servings.

Mrs. William F. Poole, III, Winter Haven, Florida

BAKED STUFFED SHRIMP

1 lb. large shrimp	1 tsp. prepared mustard
1 lb. lump crab meat	1/2 tsp. salt
2 slices bread, cubed	1 sm. onion, minced
2 tbsp. mayonnaise	1/2 green pepper, minced
1 tsp. hot sauce	1/2 c. melted butter or
1 tsp. Worcestershire sauce	margarine

Shell the shrimp, leaving the tail shells on, then split down the back and spread apart, butterfly fashion. Remove any shell particles from the crab meat and flake with a fork. Combine the crab meat, bread cubes, mayonnaise, hot sauce, Worcestershire sauce, mustard and salt. Saute the onion and green pepper in 2 tablespoons melted butter until soft, then add to the crab meat mixture. Stuff the shrimp firmly with the crab meat mixture. Place the shrimp, tail sides up, on a greased shallow baking dish and brush with the remaining butter. Bake at 400 degrees for about 15 minutes or until lightly browned. Serve with tartar sauce. 2-3 servings.

Baked Stuffed Shrimp (above)

PAPRIKA SHRIMP

2 lb. jumbo shrimp	1 tbsp. paprika
1 pkg. onion soup mix	

Shell and devein the shrimp, then place in a greased baking pan. Cover with the soup mix and 1 3/4 cup water. Sprinkle with the paprika. Bake at 350 degrees for 45 minutes or until lightly browned. 6 servings.

M. E. Knox, Miami, Florida

SHRIMP-ARTICHOKE NEWBURG

2 9-oz. packages frozen artichoke hearts	1/4 c. grated Parmesan cheese
2 12-oz. packages frozen shrimp Newburg	1 tbsp. fine dry bread crumbs

Preheat oven to 350 degrees. Cook the artichoke hearts according to package directions and drain. Place in 4 individual shallow baking dishes. Heat the shrimp Newburg according to package directions until thawed and spoon over artichoke hearts. Mix the cheese and bread crumbs and sprinkle over shrimp Newburg. Bake for about 20 minutes or until heated through.

Mrs. E. J. Wooley, Shelbyville, Tennessee

BAKED STUFFED RED SNAPPER

1 3-lb. red snapper	Dash of pepper
Butter	2 tbsp. lemon juice
1 tbsp. flour	Stuffing
2 tbsp. salt	

Wash the red snapper thoroughly. Cream 1/3 cup butter until smooth, then add the flour, salt and pepper and stir in the lemon juice. Rub the snapper inside and out with the butter mixture. Place in a baking pan. Cover and refrigerate for 30 minutes. Fill with Stuffing. Combine 2 tablespoons butter with 1/4 cup hot water. Bake, uncovered, at 350 degrees for 1 hour and 30 minutes, basting with butter mixture at 20 minute intervals.

Stuffing

2/3 c. cold water	1/2 c. chopped celery
1 1/4 c. cracker crumbs	1 tbsp. chopped green pepper
1/4 c. corn bread crumbs	1/2 c. chopped onion
3 tbsp. melted butter	1 tbsp. minced parsley
1 tsp. lemon juice	1 tsp. chopped pimento
1 egg, beaten	

Pour the water over the crumbs to moisten, then add the butter, lemon juice, egg and remaining ingredients and mix well.

Mrs. Gail Newlove, Vicksburg, Mississippi

CRAB-STUFFED RED SNAPPER

1 4-lb. red snapper	1/4 c. chopped parsley
Salt and pepper to taste	1/4 c. heavy cream
1/3 c. minced onion	1/4 tsp. thyme
3 tbsp. butter	1/3 c. melted butter
1/2 lb. crab meat	1/3 c. dry white wine
1/2 c. fresh bread crumbs	

Sprinkle the red snapper cavity with salt and pepper. Saute the onion in butter until golden, then mix in the crab meat, bread crumbs, parsley, cream and thyme. Stuff the snapper with the crab mixture and sew or skewer the edges together. Place in a greased baking pan. Combine the melted butter and wine and pour over the snapper. Bake, uncovered, for 45 minutes in a 400-degree oven, basting frequently with pan juice.

Jeanne Sommerville, Huntsville, Alabama

BAKED RED SNAPPER

1/2 c. flour	3 c. chopped canned tomatoes
Salt	1 tbsp. Worcestershire sauce
Pepper to taste	1 tbsp. catsup
1 2-lb. red snapper	1/2 lemon, sliced
6 tbsp. butter	2 bay leaves
1/2 c. chopped onion	1 clove of garlic
2 c. chopped celery	1 tsp. chili powder
1/4 c. chopped green pepper	

Combine the flour, salt and pepper and dredge the red snapper with the seasoned flour. Place in a baking pan. Combine the remaining ingredients and 1 teaspoon salt in a saucepan and bring to a boil, then simmer for 15 minutes. Pour the tomato sauce over the red snapper. Bake at 350 degrees for 45 minutes. 6 servings.

Mrs. Marvin Nunn, Blytheville, Arkansas

BAKED FILLET OF SOLE STUFFED WITH LOBSTER

3 slices bread	1/2 lb. cooked lobster,
1 tbsp. cracker crumbs	cubed
2 tbsp. sherry	4 fillets of sole
1 tbsp. grated Cheddar cheese	2 tbsp. melted butter
1/8 tsp. salt	1/2 c. milk

Preheat oven to 350 degrees. Remove the crusts from the bread slices, then coarsely crumble the bread. Combine with the cracker crumbs, sherry, cheese, salt and lobster. Spoon the stuffing mixture along 1 end of each fillet and roll up lightly. Secure with toothpicks. Arrange the rolled fillets in a flat baking pan. Pour the butter and milk over the fillets and sprinkle with additional salt. Bake in 350-degree oven for 25 minutes. Serve with Newberg sauce, if desired.

Mrs. Martha Gambrell, Richmond, Virginia

Baked Sole in White Wine (below)

BAKED SOLE IN WHITE WINE

2 lb. sole fillets	1/4 tsp. pepper
3 c. sliced cooked potatoes	1 c. sour cream
1 4-oz. can sliced mushrooms, drained	1/2 c. dry white wine
1 tsp. paprika	2 tbsp. flour
1/2 tsp. salt	1 tbsp. grated onion

Skin the fillets and cut into serving-size portions. Arrange potatoes in a well-greased 12 x 8 x 2-inch baking dish, then top with the mushrooms. Combine the paprika, salt and pepper, then sprinkle half the seasoning over the potatoes and mushrooms. Combine the sour cream, wine, flour and onion, and spread half the cream mixture over the mushrooms. Top with the fillets. Sprinkle with the remaining seasoning and spread with the remaining cream mixture. Bake at 350 degrees for 35 to 45 minutes or until fish flakes easily when tested with a fork. Remove from the oven and let stand for 10 minutes for easier serving. Garnish with watercress and sprinkle with parsley, if desired.

STUFFED TROUT

1/4 c. chopped celery	1 c. bread crumbs
1 clove of garlic, minced	Salt and pepper to taste
1/4 c. chopped green onions	4 trout fillets
2 tbsp. olive oil	Flour
1/2 c. chopped cooked shrimp	Melted butter
1/2 c. lump crab meat	

Saute the celery, garlic and onions in hot olive oil until soft. Add the shrimp and simmer for 15 minutes, stirring to prevent sticking. Add the crab meat and stir gently. Add the bread crumbs, salt and pepper. Pack the shrimp mixture on 2 trout fillets and cover with remaining fillets. Season with salt and pepper and secure with toothpicks. Dust the stuffed trout lightly with flour, then brush with melted butter. Place in a baking dish and broil until lightly browned on both sides. Add a small amount of water and brush again with melted butter. Bake at 350 degrees until tender. Place on a platter and serve with lemon butter. 2 servings.

Mrs. Alpha Hardcastle, Aransas Pass, Texas

TROUT AMANDINE

1 tsp. salt	Paprika
1 tsp. monosodium glutamate	Juice of 1 lemon
1/8 tsp. white pepper	2 tbsp. grated lemon rind
4 brook trout, cleaned	1/8 c. toasted slivered
3/4 c. melted butter	almonds

Combine the salt, monosodium glutamate, pepper and 1 cup water, then pour into a shallow baking dish. Place the trout in the baking dish and drizzle with half the butter. Sprinkle with paprika. Bake in 475-degree oven for about 15 minutes or until fish flakes easily when tested with a fork. Place on platter. Combine the remaining butter, lemon juice, lemon rind and almonds and pour over the trout. Garnish with parsley sprigs, lemon wedges and cherry tomatoes.

Mrs. Elsie Bailey, Rome, Georgia

TATER-DIPPED OVEN-FRIED FISH

2 eggs, slightly beaten	2 c. instant potato flakes
2 lb. fish fillets	1/2 c. butter
Salt and pepper to taste	2 tbsp. lemon juice

Combine the eggs and 1/4 cup water, then dip the fish in the egg mixture. Sprinkle the fish with salt and pepper and roll in potato flakes. Melt the butter in a large shallow baking pan, then stir in the lemon juice. Place the fish over the butter mixture. Bake, uncovered, at 400 degrees for 25 to 30 minutes, turning once.

Mrs. Lena Sykes, Aberdeen, Mississippi

TUNA-CHEESE LOAF

Butter or margarine	4 eggs, beaten
12 slices bread	3 c. milk
2 6 1/2-oz. cans tuna	Salt to taste
3/4 lb. grated Cheddar cheese	

Butter one side of each bread slice. Place 6 slices, buttered side down, in 9 x 13-inch pan. Drain and flake the tuna. Spread tuna over bread and sprinkle cheese over tuna. Place remaining slices of bread, buttered side up, on cheese. Mix the eggs, milk and salt and pour over bread. Let stand for 1 hour. Bake in 350-degree oven for 35 minutes or until lightly browned. Cut into 6 servings.

Mrs. Jim Masters, Tulsa, Oklahoma

TUNA ROLL

1 3/4 c. flour	1 can tuna
1/2 tsp. salt	1 sm. onion, chopped
4 tsp. baking powder	1/4 c. pickle relish
1/4 c. shortening	1 can tomato soup
1 egg, beaten	1/4 c. cheese
Milk	

Sift the flour, salt and baking powder together and cut in the shortening. Add the egg and 1/2 cup milk and mix well. Roll out the dough. Combine the tuna, 1/3 cup milk, onion and relish and spread on the dough, then roll up. Place on a greased cookie sheet. Bake at 300 degrees till brown. Combine the tomato soup and cheese in a saucepan and cook until the cheese is melted. Serve the tomato sauce over the tuna roll.

Mrs. Adelle Hart, Paris, Texas

BAKED WHITEFISH WITH DRESSING

1 whole whitefish	1/4 c. water
Salt	1 egg, beaten
1 med. onion, minced	1 tbsp. chopped green onion
1/4 c. butter	1 tbsp. chopped parsley
2 c. soft bread crumbs	Melted butter

Clean the whitefish, then rub the inside with salt. Saute the onion in melted butter. Soak the bread crumbs in the water, then add the egg. Add the bread crumb mixture to the sauteed onion and cook for about 5 minutes over low heat, stirring frequently. Remove from heat and add the green onion and parsley. Fill the whitefish with the stuffing and tie to hold the stuffing. Brush the outside with melted butter. Bake at 350 degrees for about 15 minutes per pound or until fish flakes easily when tested with fork. 4-6 servings.

Mrs. W. J. Morgan, Houston, Texas

WHITEFISH WITH DILL-CHEESE STUFFING

1 3-lb. whitefish, dressed	2 tbsp. melted butter
Dill-Cheese Stuffing	Salt and pepper to taste

Cut the whitefish in half and place one half, skin side down, in a greased large shallow baking dish. Spread with Dill-Cheese Stuffing. Place the remaining half of whitefish, skin side up, over stuffing and fasten with skewers or picks. Brush the top with butter and sprinkle with salt and pepper. Bake in 350-degree oven for 1 hour or until the whitefish flakes easily.

Dill-Cheese Stuffing

3 c. soft bread crumbs	1/2 c. chopped dill pickle
1 c. cottage cheese	1 sm. onion, chopped

1 egg, beaten   1/4 tsp. pepper
1 tsp. salt

Combine the bread crumbs, cottage cheese, pickle and onion in a medium-sized bowl. Add the egg, salt and pepper and toss lightly with a fork.

Mrs. Archie Glover, Milton, Florida

PARADE-DRESSED WHITEFISH

2 lb. whitefish fillets   Cheese Stuffing
1 tsp. salt   2 tbsp. oil
Dash of pepper   Paprika

Sprinkle the fillets with salt and pepper, then place half the fillets, skin side down, in well-greased 12 x 8 x 2-inch baking dish. Place the stuffing over the fillets, then cover with the remaining fillets. Brush with the oil and sprinkle with paprika. Bake at 350 degrees for 30 to 35 minutes or until fish flakes easily when tested with a fork.

Cheese Stuffing

1 c. chopped onion   2 tbsp. chopped parsley
1/4 c. oil   2 tsp. powdered mustard
2 c. toasted bread cubes   Dash of pepper
1 c. grated Cheddar cheese

Saute the onion in the oil until tender, then combine with the remaining ingredients and mix thoroughly.

Parade-Dressed Whitefish (above)

broiled seafood

Of the numerous methods for cooking seafood that are detailed in this book, broiling and grilling require the most careful attention by the cook. The intensity and directness of the heat often tends to dry out the fish or shellfish unless it is generously and regularly basted. As a result, whole fish, thick fish steaks, and shellfish, with their greater proportion of natural juices, are best suited for broiling or grilling. Yet, with basting, even delicate fish fillets adapt well to these dry heat methods.

Basting is the key to succulent broiled or grilled seafood. In the following chapter you will find a plentiful assortment of recipes that include tasty basting liquids and sauces. Although a particular seafood will be specified in a recipe, many other varieties of fish and shellfish can be successfully and deliciously substituted.

The simplest recipes combine herbs and seasonings with oil or butter as in Broiled Pompano with Garlic Butter, Broiled Halibut with Herbs, and Broiled Lake Trout with Almond Sauce.

You will notice that most of the recipes in this section share one common but essential feature: a basting liquid or sauce containing some fat or oil. Thus, in spite of the intense heat of the broiler or charcoal grill, you can look forward to flavorfully juicy seafood dishes.

ROCK LOBSTER WITH SAUCES

8 8-oz. South African rock lobster-tails	Chilled Red Sauce
Butter or margarine	Warm Yellow Sauce

Rinse the frozen tails under hot water, then remove the wrap and label. Insert the point of the kitchen shears between the meat and hard shell on back. Clip the hard shell down the center, leaving the tail fan intact. Do not remove the soft underside membrane of the tail. Take the tail in both hands, then open gently, peeling the shell back from the meat. Lift the tail meat through the split shell to rest on the outside of the shell. Leave the tail meat attached to the end of the shell. Arrange the tails in a shallow broiler pan, then brush with butter. Broil about 5 inches from the heat for 5 to 10 minutes or until meat is creamy white and opaque. Serve with Chilled Red Sauce or Warm Yellow Sauce.

Chilled Red Sauce

1 c. sour cream	2 tbsp. pickle relish
1/3 c. tomato juice	1 tbsp. horseradish
1/4 c. finely chopped stuffed olives	1 tsp. lemon juice
	Salt and pepper to taste

Combine all the ingredients and mix well. Chill until ready to serve. Garnish with chopped stuffed olives.

Warm Yellow Sauce

1/2 c. melted butter or margarine	Juice of 1 lemon
2 tbsp. prepared mustard	3 drops of hot sauce
	1 tsp. Worcestershire sauce

Combine all the ingredients in a small saucepan, then simmer until heated through. Serve warm, topped with finely chopped parsley.

FIVE-MINUTE BROILED SHRIMP

3 cloves of garlic, minced	Salt and pepper to taste
1/3 c. butter	1/2 lemon, thinly sliced
1 lb. deveined shrimp	

Saute the garlic in the butter for about 3 minutes. Place the shrimp in a foil-lined broiler pan. Sprinkle with salt and pepper and arrange the lemon slices over shrimp. Drizzle with the butter mixture. Broil in preheated broiler, 3 inches from source of heat, for about 5 minutes or until done, brushing once with drippings.

Mrs. Clara Knotts, Atlanta, Georgia

PAN-BROILED SHRIMP IN BUTTER

1 stick butter or margarine	2 tbsp. chopped parsley
1 c. finely chopped onions	Juice of 1 sm. lemon
2 cloves of garlic, minced	Toast
1 lb. cleaned shrimp, deveined	

Rock Lobster with Sauces (page 96)

Melt the butter in a frypan, then add the onions and saute until soft but not brown. Add the shrimp and cook for about 8 minutes or until shrimp turn pink, stirring frequently. Add the parsley and lemon juice and cook for 2 to 3 minutes longer. Serve on toast. 2 servings.

Mary Huttner, New Orleans, Louisiana

SAUCY SHRIMP CANTON

1 tbsp. butter or margarine	1/4 tsp. tarragon leaves,
1/2 c. finely chopped onion	crumbled
2 4 1/2-oz. cans lge. shrimp	1 sm. can water chestnuts
3 tbsp. prepared spicy mustard	3 or 4 California avocados
3 tbsp. lemon juice	Buttered bread crumbs
2 tbsp. soy sauce	

Melt the butter in a large skillet, then add the onion and cook over low heat until tender. Rinse the shrimp and drain. Add to the onion with the mustard, lemon juice, soy sauce and tarragon, then heat through. Drain the chestnuts and slice, then add to the onion mixture. Cut the avocados in half and remove the seed, then peel. Place the avocado halves in ovenproof dish. Heap the hot shrimp mixture in each half and sprinkle with the buttered crumbs. Broil for 1 minute or until crumbs are lightly browned. Garnish with parsley or watercress.

Photograph for this recipe on page 94.

MARINATED CHARCOALED SHRIMP

2 lb. large shrimp in shells	1 tsp. salt
3 cloves of garlic, chopped	1/2 c. olive or peanut oil
1 med. onion, chopped	3 tbsp. lemon juice
1 tsp. dry mustard	1/2 c. chopped parsley
	1 tsp. dry basil (opt.)

Rinse the shrimp in cold water, then snip shell down the back. Place in a bowl. Combine the remaining ingredients and pour over the shrimp. Marinate in the refrigerator for at least 5 hours. Drain, then arrange the shrimp on a grill over hot coals. Cook for 5 to 8 minutes, turning once. Serve in the shells with desired sauces. 4 servings.

Mrs. Richard Vaughn, Mt. Airy, North Carolina

CRUSTY SEAFOOD BROCHETTE

16 lge. shrimp, cleaned	1 tsp. paprika
16 scallops	2 tbsp. Worcestershire sauce
16 lge. fresh oysters	2 tbsp. bleu cheese
8 mushroom caps	Oil
Juice of 1 lime	

Place the shrimp, scallops, oysters and mushrooms in large dish, then add the remaining ingredients except the oil. Marinate for 4 hours in the refrigerator. Place 1 mushroom on each of 4 skewers, then arrange 4 shrimp, 4 scallops and 4 oysters on skewers. Add the remaining mushrooms to the skewers. Brush with oil. Broil for 10 minutes or until browned.

Mrs. F. L. Love, Miami, Florida

BROILED HALIBUT WITH HERBS

2 lb. 1-in. thick halibut steaks	1/4 tsp. pepper
1/3 c. butter	1/4 tsp. thyme
2 tbsp. minced onion	1/8 tsp. dried tarragon
1/2 tsp. salt	1/4 tsp. dried basil
1 clove of garlic, minced	1/4 tsp. dried parsley
	1 tbsp. lemon juice

Place halibut in foil-lined broiler pan without rack. Blend the butter, onion, seasonings and herbs together, then add the lemon juice, a small amount at a time. Spread half the herb-butter over halibut. Broil in preheated broiler, 2 inches from source of heat, for 3 to 5 minutes. Turn carefully with pancake turner, then spread the remaining herb-butter over top. Broil for 3 to 5 minutes longer or until fish flakes easily when tested with fork. Do not overcook. Remove to platter and spoon sauce in broiler over top. 4-6 servings.

Linda Thompson, Bethesda, Maryland

CHARCOAL-BROILED MACKEREL

1/2 c. melted butter	1 5 to 6-lb. mackerel
Juice of 1 lemon	Salt and pepper to taste
1 clove of garlic, minced	1 med. onion, sliced

Combine the butter, lemon juice and garlic in saucepan. Clean the mackerel and remove the head and tail. Season inside and out with salt and pepper. Place the onion in cavity. Place on grill and broil for about 25 minutes on each side or until fish flakes easily when tested with fork, basting frequently with the butter mixture. 8-10 servings.

Mrs. Melba Lewis, Pensacola, Florida

JIFFY FILLETS

2 lb. rockfish fillets	1 tsp. salt
1/4 c. oil	Dash of white pepper
2 tbsp. lemon juice	Paprika

Cut the fillets into serving-sized portions. Combine the oil, lemon juice, salt and pepper. Place the fillets, skin side up, on a well-greased broiler pan and brush with the lemon mixture. Sprinkle with paprika. Broil about 3 inches from source of heat for 4 to 5 minutes. Turn carefully and brush with the remaining lemon mixture. Sprinkle with paprika. Broil 4 to 5 minutes longer or until fish flakes easily when tested with a fork. Serve with lightly fried eggs and toasted English muffins.

Jiffy Fillets (above)

BROILED SPANISH MACKEREL FILLETS

6 Spanish mackerel fillets
Salt and pepper to taste

3 tbsp. lemon juice
Mayonnaise to taste

Place the fillets on foil on broiler rack. Sprinkle with salt, pepper and lemon juice, then spread with mayonnaise. Tuck foil up around edge to hold juices. Broil about 6 inches from source of heat for about 10 minutes or until fish flakes easily when tested with fork.

Mrs. Susan Toaz, Bradenton, Florida

BROILED POMPANO WITH GARLIC BUTTER

4 sm. pompano, cleaned
4 tbsp. mayonnaise
Salt and pepper to taste

1/2 c. melted butter
1/8 tsp. garlic powder

Cut 2 or 3 slashes with a sharp knife on each side of pompano. Rub both sides of pompano with mayonnaise, then sprinkle with salt and pepper. Place on rack of broiler pan. Combine the butter and garlic powder. Broil the pompano for about 20 minutes on each side or until fish flakes easily, turning and basting with the butter mixture. Serve with lemon wedges and any remaining butter mixture. 4 servings.

Mrs. B. L. Bevis, Lake Placid, Florida

LAZY-DAY BROILED SCALLOPS

1 lb. scallops
2 tbsp. melted butter
Juice of 2 lemons
1 tsp. Worcestershire sauce

Dash of salt
Dash of garlic salt
Paprika

Place the scallops in a shallow pan, then combine the butter, lemon juice, Worcestershire sauce, salt and garlic salt and pour over the scallops. Refrigerate until the butter solidifies. Remove from the refrigerator and sprinkle with paprika. Broil for 10 minutes or until done.

Mrs. J. A. Baldwin, Fort Myers Beach, Florida

SCHOLARLY SCALLOPS

2 lb. scallops
1 c. dry white wine
1 1/2 tsp. salt
1 sm. bay leaf
Dash of thyme

1/2 c. butter or margarine,
  melted
1 tbsp. chopped parsley
1/2 tsp. garlic salt
2 tbsp. grated Parmesan cheese

Rinse the scallops with cold water to remove any shell particles. Cut any large scallops in half. Combine 2 cups water, wine, salt, bay leaf and thyme in a large saucepan and bring to a boil. Add the scallops, then cover and simmer for 2 to 3 minutes or until the scallops are tender. Drain. Place the scallops in 6 individual shells. Combine the butter, parsley and garlic salt and pour over the scallops. Sprinkle with the cheese. Bake at 400 degrees for 15 to 20 minutes or until lightly browned. Garnish with pimento and parsley. 6 servings.

Photograph for this recipe on page 103.

BROILED SALMON

1 6-lb. salmon, dressed	Juice of 1 lemon
Salt and pepper to taste	1 clove of garlic, crushed
1/2 bottle catsup	1 tbsp. Worcestershire sauce
1/2 lb. butter, melted	

Split the salmon open along backbone, then cut out backbone. Line broiler pan with aluminum foil and place the salmon on foil. Season with salt and pepper. Place pan 4 inches from heat. Mix the remaining ingredients together. Broil the salmon for about 20 minutes, or until fish flakes easily when tested with fork, basting frequently with the catsup mixture. Do not turn the salmon. Garnish with parsley and lemon wedges.

Mrs. Mattie Jones, Houston, Texas

CHARCOAL-GRILLED RED SNAPPER FILLETS

2 lb. red snapper fillets	1/2 tsp. Worcestershire sauce
1/2 c. melted fat or oil	1/4 tsp. white pepper
1/4 c. lemon juice	Dash of hot pepper sauce
2 tsp. salt	Paprika

Place the fillets in well-greased, hinged wire grill baskets. Combine the remaining ingredients except the paprika, then baste the fish with the sauce and sprinkle with paprika. Cook about 4 inches from moderately hot coals for 8 minutes, basting with the sauce. Turn and baste with sauce, then cook for 7 to 10 minutes longer or until fish flakes easily when tested with a fork. Serve with cooked zucchini slices. Garnish with cherry tomatoes. 6 servings.

Charcoal-Grilled Red Snapper Fillets (above)

GRILLED RED SNAPPER

1/2 c. butter	1/4 tsp. onion salt
1/4 c. lemon juice	1 2-lb. red snapper
3/4 tsp. Worcestershire	Chopped parsley
sauce	

Melt the butter over low heat in a 1-quart saucepan and add the lemon juice, Worcestershire sauce and onion salt. Mix well, then remove from heat. Place the snapper in a hinged wire basket, then place on grill. Cook, basting occasionally with sauce, for 5 to 8 minutes on each side, turning once. Heat the remaining sauce. Serve with the snapper. Sprinkle with parsley. 6-8 servings.

Mrs. Margaret Knowles, Atlanta, Georgia

BROILED RED SNAPPER

1 4-lb. red snapper	Juice of 2 lemons
1 stick butter, melted	Salt and pepper to taste

Wash the red snapper and place in broiler pan. Cover with half the butter and lemon juice and sprinkle with salt and pepper. Place the pan about 6 inches from source of heat. Broil for about 20 minutes. Turn snapper and cover with remaining butter and juice. Sprinkle with salt and pepper. Broil for about 10 to 15 minutes. Turn again gently, basting the snapper and broil until lightly browned. 4-6 servings.

Vicci Willbanks, West Monroe, Louisiana

BONANZA-BROILED SEA BASS

2 lb. sea bass, cut	1 c. pineapple chunks and
3/4 in. thick	juice
2 tbsp. butter or margarine	1/2 tsp. salt

Place the bass in a broiler pan, then dot with the butter and cover with the pineapple. Sprinkle with the salt. Broil for 25 minutes or until fish flakes easily when tested with fork.

Mrs. Frank Love, Miami, Florida

BARBECUED BASS

1 onion, finely chopped	1/4 tsp. Worcestershire sauce
2 tbsp. butter	1/3 c. catsup
Juice of 1/2 lemon	Cayenne pepper to taste
2 tsp. vinegar	1 3-lb. bass, boned
1 tsp. honey	Salt to taste

Combine all the ingredients except the bass and salt in a saucepan. Simmer, stirring occasionally, until thickened. Place the bass in a greased baking pan.

Sprinkle with salt and spread with the sauce. Broil for about 20 minutes or until the bass flakes easily, basting frequently with sauce.

Mrs. Marilyn Smith, Albany, Georgia

BROILED HADDOCK

1 lb. haddock fillets	**1 onion, minced**
Salt and pepper to taste	**2 tbsp. catsup**
3 tbsp. butter	**1 tbsp. Worcestershire sauce**

Place the haddock on the rack of a broiler pan and sprinkle with salt and pepper. Melt the butter in a saucepan and add the onion, catsup and Worcestershire sauce. Stir until well blended, then spoon over the haddock. Broil for about 15 minutes on each side, basting with the onion mixture. Garnish with crisp bacon slices to serve.

Mrs. John Wilder, Auburn, Alabama

HOPSCOTCH HADDOCK

2 lb. haddock fillets	**1 tsp. salt**
2 tbsp. oil	**1/2 tsp. paprika**
2 tbsp. lemon juice	**Dash of pepper**

Place the fillets in a single layer, skin side down, on a well-greased 15 x 10 x 1-inch baking pan. Combine the remaining ingredients and mix well, then pour the sauce over the fillets. Broil about 4 inches from source of heat for 10 to 15 minutes or until fish flakes easily when tested with a fork, basting once during broiling with pan drippings. Garnish with toasted almonds and orange slices. 6 servings.

Hopscotch Haddock (above)
Scholarly Scallops (page 100)

103

TROUT MARGUERY

3 tbsp. flour	6 lb. trout fillets
6 tbsp. melted butter	Salt to taste
1 lb. boiled shrimp, chopped	Cayenne pepper to taste
1 bunch green onions, chopped	Toast
12 oysters, chopped	1/4 c. chopped parsley
1/2 c. dry white wine	

Blend the flour in the butter to form a smooth paste in a skillet. Stir the shrimp into the butter mixture, then add the onions and cook until wilted. Add the oysters and simmer for 5 minutes, then stir in the wine and remove from heat. Sprinkle the trout lightly with salt and cayenne pepper. Broil on both sides until browned. Arrange the trout on toast and cover with the shrimp mixture. Sprinkle with parsley. 12 servings.

Mrs. Janet S. Chatelain, Bunkie, Louisiana

BROILED LAKE TROUT WITH ALMOND SAUCE

4 lake trout	1/2 c. slivered almonds
3/4 c. butter, melted	Juice and grated rind of
Salt and pepper to taste	1 lemon
Paprika	

Place the trout in a skillet with just enough boiling salted water to cover. Cook for 12 minutes. Remove the trout carefully to avoid breaking and place in a shallow pan. Brush the trout with butter and sprinkle with salt and pepper. Broil for 5 minutes, basting with butter if needed to prevent drying. Sprinkle with paprika. Toast the almonds in any remaining butter and add the lemon juice and rind. Pour over the trout and serve.

Mrs. Melanie A. Scott, Louisville, Kentucky

GRILLED TROUT WITH PEACHES IN HERBED SHELLS

4 1-lb. cleaned trout	Instant minced onion
French dressing	Peaches in Herbed Shells

Remove the head and fins from the trout, then dry. Brush the cavity with the dressing, then sprinkle with the onion. Place in a well-greased, hinged wire grill basket. Brush with the dressing and place on grill over the coals. Grill until tender, turning and basting with the dressing. Serve with Peaches in Herbed Shells.

Peaches in Herbed Shells

1 c. sifted all-purpose flour	1/4 tsp. dried basil
1/2 tsp. salt	1/4 tsp. dried rosemary

1/4 tsp. dillweed
1/3 c. shortening
2 tbsp. water
1 tsp. fresh lemon juice

1   29-oz. can cling peach halves
3 tbsp. fresh lime juice
1 tbsp. soy sauce
1 tsp. instant minced onion

Sift the flour and salt into a bowl, then stir in the crumbled herbs. Cut in the shortening, then add the water and lemon juice to make a stiff dough. Round up into a ball and divide into 5 or 6 equal portions. Roll each to a circle about 4 inches in diameter. Fit over the back of large muffin pans or custard cups to make shallow shells. Shells should be about 1/2 inch deep and 3 1/2 inches wide. Place, pastry side up, on baking sheet. Prick surface of pastry with a fork. Bake at 425 degrees for about 10 to 12 minutes or until golden brown. Drain the peaches and reserve the syrup. Combine the peach syrup, lime juice, soy sauce and onion in a saucepan. Bring to a boil, then pour over the peaches. Cover and let stand for 4 or 5 hours or overnight. Drain the peaches well and place 1 peach half in each pastry shell.

FISHERMAN'S GRILLED TROUT

6 dressed trout
1/4 c. French dressing
1 tbsp. lemon juice

1 tsp. salt
1/4 tsp. pepper

Clean, wash and dry the trout. Combine the remaining ingredients and brush each trout inside and out with the sauce. Place the trout on well-greased grill. Cook over moderately hot coals for 15 to 20 minutes. Turn and brush with sauce. Grill for 15 minutes longer or until fish flakes easily when tested with fork. 6 servings.

Mrs. Maurice Goolsby, Carthage, Texas

Grilled Trout with Peaches in Herbed Shells (page 104)

Trophy Trout (page 118)

fried and sauteed seafood

The most common method of seafood cookery – frying – is one that seems to have been developed especially for fish and shellfish. It is accomplished by two basic techniques: deep-frying, in a layer of fat deep enough to float the seafood; and pan-frying and sauteeing, in only a small amount of fat. For both methods the principle is the same: on contact with the hot fat, a crust is formed and the natural juices of the fish or shellfish are sealed inside.

Successful deep-frying depends on the correct temperature of the cooking oil. For the deep-fried seafood in this section, a cooking temperature of 350 to 360 degrees is recommended. At this temperature the seafood will neither be grease-soaked nor undercooked, and you can enjoy all its crunchy goodness.

Pan-frying and sauteeing are very similar. The major difference is that sauteeing calls for butter and subsequently a lower cooking temperature. (Butter burns at a lower temperature than vegetable oil.) Pan-frying, however, usually specifies cooking oil heated to 350 degrees. Try Kitte's Portuguese Shrimp and savor the sweet buttery taste of sauteed seafood. Or enjoy crisp and juicy Fried Freshwater Bass.

Whatever method of frying seafood you prefer, you'll find in this chapter recipes representative of each of the methods. Take your pick!

107

FRIDAY FISH

Bass, well cleaned
Salt and pepper to taste

Cornmeal
Shortening

Sprinkle the bass with salt and pepper, then roll in cornmeal. Fry in shortening until golden brown and drain on paper towels. Serve with hush puppies and a green salad.

Mrs. Frank R. White, Lenoir, North Carolina

FRIED BASS

2 lb. bass, well cleaned
Lemon juice
1/2 c. cornmeal

1/2 c. flour
1 tsp. salt
1/4 tsp. pepper

Slice the bass and squeeze lemon juice on the slices. Combine the cornmeal, flour, salt and pepper, then roll the bass in the seasoned cornmeal. Fry in 2-inch deep shortening until brown, then drain.

J. T. Ashcraft, Bryan, Texas

FRIED FRESHWATER BASS

1 c. flour
1 tsp. salt
Pepper to taste

1 tsp. finely chopped onion
6 bass, dressed
Cooking oil

Mix the flour, salt and pepper well, then add the onion and mix again. Roll the bass in the flour mixture. Pour cooking oil to a depth of about 1/8 inch in a skillet and heat until bubbly, then add the bass and fry on both sides until brown.

Dora S. Williams, LaGrange, Georgia

FRIED CATFISH

2 lb. dressed catfish
Salt to taste
2 c. buttermilk

2 c. yellow cornmeal
1 lb. shortening

Cut the catfish into serving pieces and sprinkle with salt. Dip the catfish in the buttermilk and roll in the cornmeal. Fry the catfish in hot shortening in a heavy skillet until golden brown and drain on paper towels. 4 servings.

Mrs. Lila Hunter, Millington, Tennessee

BLACKFISH PATTIES

2 c. flaked cooked blackfish
1 egg, well beaten

1/2 c. cornmeal
1 med. chopped onion

Salt to taste　　　　**Liquid from boiled blackfish**
Pepper to taste

Combine the blackfish, egg, cornmeal, onion, salt and pepper and add enough liquid to moisten well. Form into patties, then fry in hot deep fat until brown.

Betty Carol Green, Bladenboro, North Carolina

BATTER-FRIED CLAMS

1 egg, beaten	2 tbsp. baking powder
3/4 c. milk	1/4 tsp. salt
1 1/3 c. sifted flour	1 pt. minced clams

Combine the egg, milk, flour, baking powder and salt. Add the clams and liquid and stir until well coated. Fry in deep 365-degree fat for 3 to 4 minutes or until brown. 4 servings.

Mrs. Irma Hoffman, Hagerstown, Maryland

FISH FRY

1 lb. fish fillets	1/4 tsp. salt
1 egg	1/2 c. fine dry bread crumbs
2 tbsp. milk	2 c. peanut oil

Wash the fish and drain. Combine the egg, milk and salt and beat until blended. Dip the fish in the egg mixture and roll in the crumbs. Fry in shallow hot 375-degree oil until golden brown. Drain fish on paper towels, then arrange on a warm platter. Garnish with parsley and lemon wedges. 4 servings.

Fish Fry (above)

CLAM FRITTERS

2 c. flour	1/2 c. clam liquid
1 tsp. baking powder	2 eggs, well beaten
Salt	24 soft clams
1 c. milk	Salt and pepper to taste

Combine the flour, baking powder, 1/2 teaspoon salt, milk, clam liquid and eggs in a shallow dish. Chop the clams and season with salt and pepper. Add the clams to the batter. Drop from a tablespoon into deep fat and fry until brown.

Mrs. W. D. Icenhour, Taylorsville, North Carolina

FRIED CLAMS

1 5-oz. can clams	1/4 c. milk
2 beaten eggs	1 c. flour
1 tsp. salt	1/2 tsp. baking powder
1/2 tsp. pepper	

Drain the clams, reserving 1/4 cup liquid. Dry the clams in a towel. Combine the eggs, salt, pepper, milk and reserved liquid. Sift the flour and baking powder together and add to the egg mixture, then beat well. Dip the clams into batter. Fry in hot fat until brown and drain on brown paper or paper towels. 4-6 servings.

Mrs. Sara Cowan, Winston-Salem, North Carolina

FRIED SOFT-SHELL CRABS

Cleaned soft-shell crabs	1/2 c. flour
Salt and pepper to taste	1/4 tsp. baking powder
1/2 c. cornmeal	Cooking oil

Season the crabs with salt and pepper and let stand for 10 minutes. Combine the cornmeal, flour and baking powder and dip the crabs in the cornmeal mixture. Fry in hot deep oil until brown.

Mrs. Howard Andersen, McLean, Virginia

CRAB PATTIES

1 tsp. minced onion	1/2 tsp. Worcestershire
2 tsp. finely chopped celery	sauce
Butter	1 c. crab meat
3 tbsp. flour	1/2 c. soft bread crumbs
3/4 c. milk	Paprika
2 eggs, beaten	Salad oil

Saute the onion and celery in butter. Melt 3 tablespoons butter in a saucepan and blend in the flour. Add the milk, gradually and cook until thick, stirring constantly. Cool and add the onion, celery, 1 egg and Worcestershire sauce. Mix thoroughly, then fold in the crab meat. Chill and mold into oblong patties. Roll in remaining egg and cover with bread crumbs. Season with paprika, then chill until ready to use. Deep fry in hot oil until brown on both sides. Serve with tartar sauce. 4 servings.

Mrs. Roselle Glazer, Chevy Chase, Maryland

SEAFOOD FONDUE

2 lb. shrimp	1/4 tsp. garlic powder
1 lb. scallops	1/4 tsp. oregano
1 lb. fish fillets	1/4 tsp. hot sauce
1 qt. cooking oil	1/4 tsp. thyme
1 8-oz. can tomato sauce	1/8 tsp. sugar
1/4 c. chili sauce	Dash of basil

Peel the shrimp, leaving the tail section, then rinse and devein. Rinse the scallops and cut large ones in half. Refrigerate all the seafood in a covered dish until 30 minutes before serving time. Drain well and pat dry with paper towels. Pour the cooking oil into a fondue cooker to 2-inch depth or not more than 1/2 full. Heat the oil to 375 degrees and maintain the temperature. Spear the seafood with a fondue fork and fry in hot oil until lightly browned. Combine all the remaining ingredients for sauce in a saucepan and simmer for 10 to 20 minutes, stirring occasionally, then serve with the seafood.

Seafood Fondue (above)

EASY FRIED SHRIMP

2 lb. jumbo shrimp	2 eggs
1 c. flour	1 c. milk
1 tsp. baking powder	Cooking oil
1 tsp. salt	

Clean and devein the shrimp and dry on a towel. Combine the flour, baking powder, salt, eggs and milk in a mixing bowl and beat vigorously. Dip the shrimp in the batter and fry in deep hot oil until golden brown.

Mrs. George A. Reid, Clinton, South Carolina

FRENCH-FRIED SHRIMP WITH ALMONDS

1 lb. large shrimp	1/2 tsp. garlic salt
1 egg	1/8 tsp. pepper
1/2 c. milk	1/4 c. chopped blanched
3/4 c. flour	almonds
1/4 tsp. crushed oregano	

Remove shells from the shrimp, leaving the last section of the shell and tail. Devein, then slice each shrimp along vein deeply enough to lay out flat, butterfly fashion. Beat the egg, milk, flour and seasonings together until smooth. Dip the shrimp in the batter and allow to drain. Spread in a single layer on a tray and sprinkle with almonds. Chill for 2 hours. Cook in deep fat at 370 degrees until golden brown.

Sarah E. Alger, Deming, New Mexico

FRENCH-FRIED SHRIMP WITH PLUM DUCK SAUCE

2 lb. fresh shrimp	1 egg, beaten
1 c. flour	1 c. ice water
1/2 tsp. sugar	2 tbsp. oil
1/2 tsp. salt	Plum Duck Sauce

Peel shells from the shrimp, leaving last section and tail intact. Devein shrimp, then cut slit through center back. Spread out shrimp in butterfly fashion, then dry thoroughly. Combine remaining ingredients for batter, then dip the shrimp in the batter. Fry in deep hot fat until golden. Drain on paper and serve immediately with Plum Duck Sauce.

Plum Duck Sauce

1 c. plum preserves	1 tbsp. sugar
1/2 c. chutney	

Combine all ingredients in saucepan and simmer for several minutes. Cool. 4 servings.

Mrs. Vincent F. Callahan, Jr., McLean, Virginia

FRIED FROGS' LEGS

8 frogs' legs	Pepper to taste
Salt	1 egg, beaten
1/2 c. lemon juice	Cracker crumbs

Skin the frogs' legs. Combine 4 cups water, 1 tablespoon salt and the lemon juice in a saucepan and bring to a boil. Scald the frogs' legs in the boiling mixture for about 2 minutes, then drain and dry. Sprinkle the frogs' legs with salt and pepper, then dip in the egg and roll in the cracker crumbs. Fry in hot deep fat for about 3 minutes or until brown.

Mrs. Walter Jones, Houston, Texas

FILLET OF HADDOCK

6 fillets of haddock	1 tbsp. minced chives
Salt and pepper to taste	1/2 c. bread crumbs
2 tbsp. lemon juice	1 egg, beaten
1 tbsp. minced parsley	1/2 c. milk

Sprinkle the fillets with salt, pepper and lemon juice. Mix the parsley and chives with the bread crumbs. Mix the egg and milk together. Dip each fillet in the milk mixture, then roll in the bread crumbs. Fry in deep fat until golden brown. Drain well and serve on hot platter with Epicurean Sauce.

Epicurean Sauce

1/2 c. heavy cream	1 tbsp. powdered horseradish
3 tbsp. mayonnaise	1/8 tsp. salt
1 tsp. mustard	Dash of cayenne pepper

Beat the cream until stiff, then stir in the mayonnaise, mustard, horseradish, salt and cayenne pepper.

Bessie Bailey, Kingsport, Tennessee

BATTER-FRIED HALIBUT

Halibut fillets	1 1/2 tsp. baking powder
Milk	2 tbsp. melted shortening
1 c. flour	1 egg
1/2 tsp. salt	

Soak the halibut in milk for 30 minutes. Combine the flour, salt, baking powder, shortening, egg and 3/4 cup milk to make a batter. Remove the halibut from the milk and dip in the batter. Fry in hot fat until brown and well done.

Mrs. Imogene Burgess, Louisa, Kentucky

Pan-Fried Oysters (below)

PAN-FRIED OYSTERS

2 12-oz. cans fresh oysters	1 1/2 c. dry bread crumbs
2 eggs, beaten	1 1/2 c. flour
2 tbsp. milk	Lemon wedges
1 tsp. salt	Quick Tartar Sauce
Dash of pepper	

Drain the oysters. Combine the egg, milk and seasonings. Combine the crumbs and flour, then roll the oysters in the crumb mixture. Dip in the egg mixture and roll again in the crumb mixture. Fry in hot fat over medium heat until brown on one side. Turn carefully and brown the other side. Drain on paper towels. Serve with lemon wedges and Quick Tartar Sauce.

Quick Tartar Sauce

1 c. mayonnaise or salad dressing	1/2 c. undrained sweet pickle relish

Combine the mayonnaise and relish and mix well. Chill thoroughly.

FRENCH-FRIED OYSTERS

1 lge. can fresh oysters	2 c. buttermilk
Salt and pepper to taste	2 c. cracker meal
2 c. flour	

Sprinkle the oysters with salt and pepper. Dip in the flour and buttermilk, then roll in the cracker meal. Drop in deep fat and fry until golden brown. Drain on paper towels. 4 servings.

Mrs. Nancy Myers, Corbin, Kentucky

GOLDEN-FRIED OYSTERS

Salad oil	1/2 tsp. pepper
2 eggs, beaten	3 doz. oysters, drained
1/4 c. oyster liquid	1 1/2 c. all-purpose flour
1/2 tsp. salt	2 c. cornmeal

Pour 1 inch of salad oil in a large heavy skillet and heat to 375 degrees. Combine the eggs, oyster liquid, salt and pepper. Dip the oysters, one at a time, in the flour, coating well. Dip in the egg mixture and then in the cornmeal, coating well. Fry until golden on both sides. Drain well on paper towels and place in a warm oven until all oysters are cooked.

Mrs. Edna M. Zerbe, Birmingham, Alabama

LITTLE OYSTER PIES

1 recipe pastry	1/4 tsp. salt
6 oysters	2 tsp. butter

Roll out pastry on a lightly floured board and cut into 6 squares. Place 1 oyster on each square, then sprinkle with salt and dot with butter. Fold over dough to make triangles and pinch the edges together to seal tightly. Fry for 3 to 5 minutes or until lightly brown. Drain on paper towels and serve immediately.

Julia Leet, St. Francisville, Louisiana

OYSTER FRITTERS

1 1/3 c. flour	2/3 c. oyster liquid
1 1/2 tsp. baking powder	2 eggs, well beaten
1/2 tsp. salt	1 c. drained oysters

Sift the flour, baking powder and salt together into a bowl, then blend in the liquid and eggs. Chop the oysters, then stir into the batter. Drop from a tablespoon into hot fat and fry for 2 to 5 minutes or until brown. 4-6 servings.

Mrs. Florence Gordon, Chattanooga, Tennessee

SALMON PATTIES

1 can salmon	1/8 tsp. pepper
1/2 c. soft bread crumbs	Dry bread crumbs
1 egg, beaten	Oil
1/8 tsp. salt	

Flake the salmon and remove the small bones. Combine the salmon, bread crumbs, egg, salt and pepper in a bowl and shape into 6 patties. Dip into the dry bread crumbs and fry in hot deep oil until golden brown. 2 servings.

Verna Leaman, Cape Coral, Florida

Family-Style Salmon Croquettes (below)

FAMILY-STYLE SALMON CROQUETTES

1 1-lb. can salmon	1/2 tsp. salt
1/4 c. butter or margarine	1/4 tsp. pepper
1 med. onion, finely chopped	1 tbsp. Worcestershire sauce
1 med. green pepper, finely	1 egg
chopped	2 tbsp. milk
1/4 c. flour	3/4 c. corn flake crumbs
1 c. mashed potatoes	

Drain the salmon and reserve the liquid. Flake the salmon and set aside. Melt the butter in a saucepan, then add the onion and green pepper and saute for 10 minutes. Stir in the flour. Remove from heat and stir in the reserved salmon liquid. Cook over low heat until mixture leaves sides of pan, stirring constantly. Beat in the potatoes, salt, pepper and Worcestershire sauce, then stir in the salmon. Cool, then chill thoroughly. Shape into croquettes. Beat the egg with the milk, then dip the croquettes in the egg mixture and coat thoroughly with the crumbs. Fry in deep fat at 365 degrees for about 5 minutes or until golden brown. Drain on absorbent paper. Serve on a bed of cooked peas. 6 servings.

SALMON-POTATO CUTLETS

1 lge. can salmon	1 1/2 tsp. salt
2 c. mashed potatoes	1/4 tsp. pepper
2 eggs	Fine bread crumbs

Remove the bones and skin from the salmon, then flake with a fork. Combine the salmon, potatoes, 1 beaten egg, salt and pepper in a bowl and mix well, then form into cutlets. Place the remaining egg in a shallow bowl and beat well. Roll the salmon cutlets in crumbs and then in the beaten egg. Roll in crumbs again. Fry in deep fat at 385 degrees for 4 to 5 minutes or until brown. 4 servings.

Bettye Robinson, Dallas, Texas

FRIED SEA SCALLOPS

1 qt. scallops	1 tsp. salt
2 eggs, slightly beaten	Dash of paprika
1/2 c. flour	

Wash and drain the scallops, then pat dry. Dip the scallops in the eggs. Combine the flour, salt and paprika in a shallow bowl and mix well. Roll the scallops in the seasoned flour. Fry in deep hot fat until golden brown and drain on paper towels. Serve with tartar sauce. 6 servings.

Kathryn Elwert, Witchita Falls, Texas

SCALLOPS GOURMET

1 pt. scallops	1 c. fine dry bread crumbs
1/2 c. flour	Corn oil
1 c. mayonnaise	

Cut large scallops in half. Roll the scallops in the flour and coat evenly with the mayonnaise. Roll in the bread crumbs. Fill a deep kettle 1/3 full with oil and heat to 375 degrees. Fry the scallops in the hot oil for 3 minutes or until golden and drain on paper towels. 4-5 servings.

Marlyn Koncaba, Hallettsville, Texas

CRUSTY TROUT

2 c. pancake mix	2 eggs
4 1-lb. trout	2 tsp. salt

Place the pancake mix in a shallow dish and coat the trout with the mix. Lift out the trout and place on waxed paper. Beat the eggs with the salt. Combine 1 cup cold water with remaining pancake mix and blend together. Roll the trout in the batter. Fry in deep fat for 5 minutes or until brown. 4 servings.

Mrs. Wilma Mordecai, Fernbank, Alabama

TROUT SUPREME

1 3/4 c. lemon-lime carbonated beverage	1 c. pancake mix
1 tsp. salt	2 1/2 lb. trout fillets

Mix the carbonated beverage, salt and pancake mix together and dip the trout in the batter. Fry the trout in fat at 375 degrees until golden brown.

Mrs. Sammy Taylor, Doerun, Georgia

TROPHY TROUT

3 lb. dressed rainbow trout	1 c. flour
1 c. buttermilk	Lemon wedges
1 pkg. onion soup mix	Watercress

Pat the trout dry with a paper towel, then place in a single layer in a shallow baking dish. Combine the buttermilk and soup mix. Brush the trout inside with the buttermilk mixture then pour the remaining buttermilk mixture over the trout and let stand for 1 hour. Remove the trout from the buttermilk mixture and roll in flour. Fry the trout in hot fat at moderate heat for 4 to 5 minutes or until brown. Turn carefully and fry for 4 to 5 minutes longer or until brown and fish flakes easily when tested with a fork. Drain on absorbent paper. Garnish with lemon wedges and watercress. 6 servings.

Photograph for this recipe on page 106.

CRISPY-FRIED RAINBOW TROUT

1/4 c. evaporated milk	1/2 c. yellow cornmeal
1 1/2 tsp. salt	1/2 tsp. paprika
Dash of pepper	6 10-oz. dressed rainbow
1/2 c. flour	trout

Combine the milk, salt and pepper, then combine the flour, cornmeal and paprika. Dip the trout in the milk mixture, then roll in the flour mixture. Fry in hot fat over medium heat for 4 to 5 minutes or until brown. Turn carefully and fry for 4 to 5 minutes longer or until brown and fish flakes easily when tested with a fork. Drain on absorbent paper. Garnish with parsley, olives and lemon wedges and serve immediately.

Crispy-Fried Rainbow Trout (above)

MOUNTAIN TROUT WITH ALMONDS

1 stick butter	1/2 c. slivered almonds
4 trout	1 tsp. chopped chives
Flour	Juice of 1 lemon

Melt the butter in a heavy skillet. Coat the trout well with flour. Place in the butter and fry until browned. Turn and brown again and remove from the butter. Reduce heat to low, then add the almonds, chives and lemon juice to the skillet. Saute until almonds are golden. Pour over trout and serve. 4 servings.

Beverly Sadler, Oklahoma City, Oklahoma

GINGER TROUT

Trout, dressed	Prepared biscuit mix
Milk	Cooking oil
1 tsp. powdered ginger	

Cut the trout in small pieces and place in a bowl. Add enough milk to cover the trout, then stir in the ginger. Let the trout marinate for about 1 hour. Combine the biscuit mix and enough water to make the consistency of pancake batter. Keep ice cold by placing the bowl of batter in a bowl of ice cubes. Remove the trout from the marinade and dry on paper towels. Dip the pieces in the cold batter and fry in deep oil at 450 degrees for about 5 minutes or until brown.

Mrs. R. W. Harper, Harlingen, Texas

MARYLAND CRAB CAKES

2 eggs, well beaten	3 c. crab meat
2 tbsp. mayonnaise	Flour
Salt and pepper to taste	4 tbsp. cooking oil
Dash of Worcestershire sauce	

Combine the eggs, mayonnaise, seasonings and crab meat and mix lightly. Add enough flour to make the crab mixture easy to handle and shape into patties. Dust lightly with flour, then saute in hot oil in a skillet until golden brown. 3-4 servings.

Mrs. Lilian B. Gardner, Tampa, Florida

MULLET FILLETS

1 1/2 lb. mullet fillets	3/4 tbsp. salt
1 egg	1 c. fine bread crumbs
1 tbsp. water	

Cut the mullet in serving pieces. Combine the egg, water and salt in a shallow bowl and beat well. Dip the mullet in the egg mixture and roll in the crumbs. Saute the mullet in hot fat in a frying pan until done and golden brown on both sides. Drain on absorbent paper. Garnish with lemon and parsley.

Mrs. Priscilla Childers, Cullman, Alabama

TUNA BALLS

1 lge. can tuna	1/4 c. evaporated milk
2 eggs	1 tbsp. Worcestershire sauce
Salt and pepper to taste	36 round buttery crackers
2 tbsp. all-purpose flour	Cooking oil

Drain and break up the tuna in a mixing bowl, then add 1 egg, salt and pepper. Blend in the flour, milk and Worcestershire sauce. Crush 24 crackers and add to the tuna mixture. Beat the remaining egg in a shallow bowl and crush the remaining crackers. Shape the tuna mixture into round balls and roll in egg, then in cracker crumbs. Fry in 2 inches cooking oil until brown on all sides. Drain on paper towels and serve hot.

Mrs. W. W. Taylor, Laurel, Mississippi

ISLAND-FRIED WHITEFISH

2 1/2 to 3 lb. whitefish fillets	3 tsp. baking powder
1/2 c. soy sauce	1 tsp. salt
1/2 c. flour	1/2 tsp. pepper
Cornstarch	2 No. 2 cans pineapple chunks
1 c. milk	3/4 c. sugar
1 egg	Cooking oil

Wash the fillets and pat dry, then cut into 1 1/2-inch squares. Marinate in soy sauce for 20 to 30 minutes, turning occasionally. Combine the flour, 1/2 cup cornstarch, milk, egg, baking powder and seasonings to make a thin batter. Pour the pineapple and syrup into a saucepan, then stir in the sugar and cook until heated through. Pour the cooking oil into a heavy skillet to a depth of 1 1/2 inches and heat to 375 degrees. Drain the whitefish squares, then dip quickly into the batter. Plunge the whitefish into the hot oil. Keep the oil at 375 degrees. Cook the whitefish until crisp and golden, then place on paper toweling and keep warm. Mix 1 tablespoon cornstarch with 1/4 cup water and add to the pineapple mixture. Cook and stir until thickened. Arrange the pineapple sauce on a warm serving platter. Place the whitefish pieces on top. 6 servings.

Mrs. Wilford Anderson, Odessa, Texas

MARINATED FROGS' LEGS

1/2 c. cider vinegar	4 pr. frogs' legs
1 bay leaf, crumbled	Flour
1 tbsp. chopped parsley	1/4 c. butter
1 sm. onion, minced	Salt to taste

Combine the first 4 ingredients in a shallow dish. Place the frogs' legs in the vinegar mixture and marinate overnight in the refrigerator. Spoon the marinade over the frogs' legs several times. Drain and wipe dry. Roll in the flour and saute in the butter over low heat until brown on both sides. Season with salt and serve hot. 4 servings.

Mrs. Josie Mathews, Oxford, Mississippi

PERCH-POTATO PANCAKES

1 lb. frozen ocean perch fillets, thawed	1 tbsp. chopped parsley
3 eggs, beaten	2 tsp. salt
2 tbsp. flour	Dash of nutmeg
2 tbsp. grated onion	Dash of pepper
	2 c. finely grated potatoes

Skin the fillets and chop fine. Add remaining ingredients and mix thoroughly. Heat a well-greased griddle or frypan until hot but not smoking. Drop 1/3 cup perch mixture on griddle and flatten slightly with a spatula. Fry for 3 to 4 minutes or until brown. Turn carefully and fry for 3 to 4 minutes longer. Drain on absorbent paper and keep warm until ready to serve. Repeat with remaining perch mixture. Serve with applesauce. 12 pancakes.

Mrs. Edgar Marven, Sr., Louisville, Kentucky

ROCK LOBSTER IN GARLIC BUTTER

12 2-oz. South African rock lobster-tails	1/4 c. minced parsley
1/2 c. butter or margarine	1/4 tsp. crumbled oregano
2 cloves of garlic, chopped	1/4 c. grated Parmesan cheese

Cut the lobster-tails while frozen through the shell into 4 crosswise pieces. Melt the butter in a large skillet, then add the garlic, parsley, oregano and lobster pieces. Cook over medium heat, stirring, for about 10 minutes or until lobster shell is red and the meat is white and opaque. Sprinkle with the cheese and serve hot with Italian bread slices. 6 servings.

Rock Lobster in Garlic Butter (above)

SALMON AND CORN FRITTERS

1 1-lb. can salmon	2 tbsp. chopped onion
1 c. canned whole kernel	1/4 tsp. salt
corn, drained	1/8 tsp. pepper
2 eggs, slightly beaten	3/4 c. coarse cracker crumbs
1/4 c. catsup	

Drain and flake the salmon, then combine with remaining ingredients. Form into 12 patties. Saute in a small amount of fat for about 1 minute and 30 seconds on each side or until golden brown. 6 servings.

Mrs. John Bishop, Birmingham, Alabama

SALMON-BACON ROLLS

1 lge. can salmon	1/3 c. evaporated milk
12 saltine crackers	6 slices bacon
1 egg, beaten	

Remove the skin and bones from the salmon and flake with a fork. Crush the crackers with a rolling pin. Combine the salmon, cracker crumbs, egg and milk and shape into 6 equal-sized rolls. Wrap each roll diagonally with a bacon slice and secure with a toothpick. Saute in a frying pan over low heat until brown and heated through. Add liquid smoke, if desired. 6 servings.

Mrs. Eva Stutler, Waco, Texas

SHRIMP PORTUGUESE

2 lb. fresh shrimp	3/4 tsp. salt
1 clove of garlic, minced	1/8 tsp. pepper
1/2 c. butter	1/2 c. minced parsley

Shell and devein the shrimp, then dry on paper towels. Saute the garlic in the butter in a frying pan until brown, then discard the garlic. Add the shrimp and saute until underside turns pink. Turn and saute until remaining side is pink. Add salt, pepper and parsley. 6 servings.

Mrs. Arthur A. Nelson, Baltimore, Maryland

SHERRY SHRIMP

1 lb. fresh shrimp	1 c. chicken bouillon
1 tbsp. sherry	2 tbsp. cornstarch
1/4 tsp. ginger	1 tbsp. cold water
3 tbsp. oil	1 can mushroom soup
1 tsp. salt	Cooked rice
1 pkg. frozen peas	

Shell and devein the shrimp, then cut the shrimp in 1/2-inch pieces. Sprinkle the shrimp pieces with the sherry and ginger. Saute the shrimp in 2 tablespoons hot oil in a frypan for about 5 minutes or until pink. Add the salt and remove the shrimp from the frypan. Add remaining oil to the frypan and saute peas until thawed. Add the bouillon and bring to a boil. Blend the cornstarch with the water and add to the bouillon mixture. Cook until the sauce is thick and clear, then add the soup and shrimp. Bring to a boil over high heat, then remove from heat immediately and serve with rice. 6 servings.

Mrs. Virginia Parkhill, Harrison, Arkansas

CHINESE SHRIMP WITH RIPE OLIVES

1 lb. deveined shrimp	1 can chicken broth
1 clove of garlic, crushed	2 tbsp. cornstarch
1/4 tsp. powdered ginger	2 tbsp. soy sauce
2 tbsp. oil	1 c. pitted California ripe
1/2 lb. ground lean pork	olives
1/2 c. diagonally sliced	1/4 c. chopped green onion
celery	

Saute the shrimp with the garlic and ginger in the oil for 1 minute. Shape the ground pork into very small balls, then add to the shrimp mixture and cook for 2 to 3 minutes. Add the celery and 1 cup broth. Bring to a boil and cover, then simmer for 10 minutes. Blend the cornstarch with the remaining broth and soy sauce, then stir into the shrimp mixture. Add the olives and green onion. Cook, stirring, until sauce thickens. Serve with steamed rice. 4 servings.

Chinese Shrimp with Ripe Olives (above)

123

Pineapple Shrimp En Croustades (page 132)

steamed, boiled, and poached seafood

Steaming, boiling, and poaching are the methods of cooking seafood that involve a boiling or simmering liquid. They have the major advantage of preserving the natural juiciness of the seafood, providing it is not overcooked. As an added feature, a subtle blending of flavors occurs when the natural seafood juices mingle with the bubbling liquid.

The technique of steaming depends on the intense heat of water vapor rather than actual physical contact with a boiling liquid. Shellfish, in particular, benefit deliciously from steaming. The edible portions, being securely encased in a natural protective covering, are cooked while the flavorful juices remain locked inside.

In boiling seafood, a greater amount of boiling liquid is used than with either steaming or poaching. As a result, the cooking seafood imparts more of its own delicate flavoring to the liquid. Shrimp Creole is just such a dish.

The culinary essence of poaching requires that only a minimum of water be used in order to preserve a maximum of flavor. Thus, the poaching liquid also becomes a seasoning agent for the seafood. Anything from white wine or vinegar to milk is recommended; often gentle touches of herbs and spices are added.

For incomparably succulent seafood dishes, you will often want to rely on this chapter.

CRAB MEAT CONSTANTINE

1 lge. onion, chopped	1 lb. lump crab meat
1 green pepper, cut in	4 pimentos, cut in
1-in. pieces	1-in. pieces
1 1/2 sticks butter	Salt and pepper to taste
1/2 c. wine	

Saute the onion and green pepper in the butter, then stir in the wine, crab meat, pimentos and seasonings. Cover and steam until onion and green pepper are tender. May be served with rice, if desired. 4-6 servings.

Mrs. W. Chandler Mosley, Jackson, Mississippi

KING CRAB DISH

1 pkg. frozen King crab,	2 tbsp. cooking sherry
thawed	1 can shrimp soup
2/3 c. mayonnaise	1 can cream of celery soup
2 tbsp. lemon juice	

Drain the crab meat. Combine remaining ingredients in blazer pan of chafing dish over hot water. Add the crab meat and cook over low heat until thoroughly heated. Serve over rice, if desired.

Mrs. Pearl Breeland, Hattiesburg, Mississippi

STEAMED LOBSTER WITH CURRY BUTTER

1 live lobster	1/4 tsp. curry powder
2 tbsp. melted butter	

Place the lobster on a rack in a large kettle and pour in 1 inch boiling water. Cover and steam for 15 to 20 minutes or until lobster turns pink. Place the lobster on a cutting board on back, then split lengthwise with a heavy sharp knife, running from the mouth through the body and tail. Remove the dark sac vein and crack large claws. Blend the butter and curry powder together and serve with the lobster.

Mrs. Violet Swanson, Dover, Delaware

SHRIMP TARRAGON WITH PIMENTO RICE

2 tbsp. butter or margarine,	1/2 tsp. tarragon
melted	1/2 tsp. seasoned pepper
3 tbsp. flour	1/2 tsp. salt
1 10-oz. can frozen cream of	1/2 tsp. onion powder
shrimp soup, thawed	1 1-lb. 4-oz. package frozen
1/2 c. chicken broth	shrimp
1/2 c. sauterne	Pimento Rice
2 tbsp. lemon juice	

Blend the butter and flour until smooth, then stir in the soup, broth, sauterne, lemon juice and seasonings. Cook, stirring constantly, until thickened. Add the shrimp and cook for 5 to 10 minutes longer. Turn in a serving dish. Garnish with fresh parsley. Serve with Pimento Rice.

Pimento Rice

1 c. chopped onions	3 c. cooked rice
2 tbsp. butter or margarine	1/4 c. diced pimento

Saute the onions in butter until tender, then add the rice and pimento. Cook until heated through.

Photograph for this recipe on cover.

PEANUT BUTTER-SAUCED SOLE FILLETS

2 lb. sole fillets	1/4 c. chunky peanut butter
Salt to taste	1 tbsp. lemon juice
1/2 c. mayonnaise or salad	2 tsp. instant minced onion
dressing	Chopped peanuts

Wipe the fillets with a damp cloth, then sprinkle with salt. Roll up and fasten with toothpicks or skewers. Place on rack above simmering water. Cover and steam for 12 to 15 minutes or until fillets are opaque. Blend the mayonnaise, peanut butter, lemon juice and onion together until smooth. Let stand for several minutes. Place the fillets in a serving dish, then spread the sauce over the top. Sprinkle with chopped peanuts, if desired. Serve at once. 6 servings.

Peanut Butter-Sauced Sole Fillets (above)

OYSTERS ROZANNE

1 1/2 tbsp. flour	2 tbsp. cold water
1 1/2 tsp. salt	1 pt. oysters
Dash of pepper	1/4 c. butter or margarine
1 tsp. Worcestershire	3 c. milk
sauce (opt.)	1 c. light cream
Few drops of hot sauce	

Combine the flour, salt, pepper, Worcestershire sauce, hot sauce and water in chafing dish blazer pan and blend to a smooth paste. Stir in the oysters and liquid. Add the butter and cook, stirring, over very low heat for about 5 minutes or until edges of oysters curl. Scald the milk and cream in a saucepan and stir into oyster mixture. Cover pan and place blazer pan over hot water. Garnish with paprika. 3-4 servings.

Willie Nicewander, Pulaski, Virginia

SCALLOPS IN CHEESE SAUCE

1/4 c. chopped celery	Salt and pepper to taste
1/4 c. chopped green pepper	1 c. milk
1/4 c. chopped onion	1 c. grated cheese
2 tbsp. butter	1 1/2 lb. scallops, drained
2 tbsp. flour	2 tbsp. sherry
1/2 tsp. dry mustard	

Saute the celery, green pepper and onion slightly in butter but do not brown. Add the flour, mustard, salt and pepper and blend well. Add the milk slowly and cook until thickened, stirring constantly. Stir in cheese until melted. Add the scallops and sherry, then cover and steam for about 10 minutes. Serve over Chinese noodles, if desired.

Mrs. J. W. Barnitz, Arlington, Virginia

SPICY ROCK LOBSTER BOIL

3 bay leaves	2 cloves of garlic
1 tbsp. whole allspice	2 lemons, sliced
1 1/2 tsp. crushed red peppers	1/4 c. salt
2 tsp. peppercorns	3 8-oz. packages South
2 tsp. whole cloves	African rock lobster-tails
2 qt. water	Sauce Complet
2 med. onions, sliced	

Tie the bay leaves and spices in a piece of cheesecloth and place in a large kettle. Add the water, onions, garlic, lemons and salt, then bring to a boil. Add the lobster-tails and return to the boiling point, then simmer for 5 minutes. Remove from heat and let stand in spiced water for 3 minutes. Drain and chill thoroughly. Cut away the underside membrane and remove lobster meat from shells in 1 piece. Slice and return slices to shells. Garnish with lemon slices and hard-boiled eggs. Serve with Sauce Complet.

Sauce Complet

4 tbsp. mayonnaise
4 tbsp. Worcestershire sauce
4 tbsp. catsup
1 tsp. horseradish

1/4 tsp. garlic juice
1/2 tsp. salt
1/8 tsp. pepper

Combine all the ingredients and chill thoroughly. Garnish with grated hard-cooked egg yolks on top just before serving, if desired.

Photograph for this recipe on page 5.

KING CRAB IN SHELLS

3 shallots
3 tbsp. butter
1 c. dry white wine
1/2 c. cream

2 tbsp. cornstarch
Salt and white pepper to taste
1 lb. King crab claw meat
Buttered bread crumbs

Slice the shallots and part of the green tops, then saute lightly in the butter. Add the wine and bring to a boil. Add the cream then stir in the cornstarch. Season with salt and pepper. Cook, stirring, until thickened. Cut the crab meat into small pieces, then stir into the sauce. Spoon into crab shells and sprinkle with bread crumbs. Bake at 450 degrees until crumbs are browned.

King Crab in Shells (above)

ROCK LOBSTER WITH CREAMY RUSSIAN SAUCE

9 6-oz. frozen South African
   rock lobster-tails
1/2 c. margarine, melted
1 pkg. creamy Russian salad
   dressing mix

2 c. sour cream
2 tbsp. lemon or lime juice
1/4 tsp. angostura aromatic
   bitters

Drop the frozen rock lobster-tails into boiling, salted water, then bring to a boil. Reduce the heat and cook for 8 minutes. Drain immediately, then drench with cold water and cut away underside membrane with kitchen scissors. Insert fingers between shell and meat at meaty end of tail and pull firmly to remove meat in 1 piece. Chill thoroughly. Combine the remaining ingredients and mix thoroughly. Place in bowl in center of large tray and serve as dip sauce. Arrange the lobster-tails on tray and garnish with cucumber slices and hard-boiled egg slices.

ROCK LOBSTER SUPREME

6 frozen rock lobster-tails
3 onions, diced
1/4 c. butter
1/2 clove of garlic, diced
3 tomatoes, peeled and diced
2 tbsp. curry powder

1 sm. stick cinnamon,
   crushed
1 bay leaf, crumbled
3 cloves, crushed
1 tsp. salt

Drop the frozen lobster-tails into boiling salted water, then return to a boil and simmer for 6 minutes. Drain the lobster-tails and drench with cold water. Cut along each edge of the membrane on the underside of the shell and strip off the membrane. Remove the lobster meat from the shells, keeping the shells intact. Dice the lobster meat. Saute the onions in the butter, then add the garlic and tomatoes. Stir in curry powder, cinnamon, bay leaf and cloves and simmer for 30 minutes. Add a small amount of butter if mixture is too dry. Add salt and lobster and mix thoroughly, then place mixture in the lobster shells. Serve immediately.

Mrs. Ray Gateley, McKenzie, Tennessee

ASPARAGUS AND SHRIMP ORIENTAL

2 c. cooked asparagus
2 tbsp. salad oil
1 med. onion, sliced
1 c. sliced celery
1/2 tsp. salt
1/4 tsp. pepper
2 tbsp. sugar

1 lb. cooked shrimp, deveined
1 4-oz. can sliced
   mushrooms, drained
1 can water chestnuts, sliced
2 tbsp. soy sauce
1 11-oz. can mandarin
   oranges, drained

Drain asparagus and set aside. Pour the oil into an electric skillet, then add the onion, celery, salt, pepper and sugar. Cook until the vegetables are crisp tender.

Rock Lobster with Creamy Russian Sauce (page 130)

Arrange the asparagus, shrimp, mushrooms and chestnuts over the cooked vegetables and sprinkle the soy sauce. Place the orange slices on top. Cover the skillet and steam for about 15 minutes. Serve on mounds of hot rice. 6 servings.

Mrs. Eva G. Key, Mount Pleasant, South Carolina

EASY BOILED SHRIMP

1 box shrimp boil seasonings	Juice of 2 lemons
1 tbsp. salt	5 lb. shrimp
1 lge. onion, chopped	

Combine the shrimp boil seasonings, salt, onion, lemon juice and 2 quarts boiling water in a large kettle. Add the shrimp, then return to a boil and boil for about 5 minutes or until the shrimp are pink. Drain well, then shell and devein. Chill the shrimp until ready to serve. 4 servings.

Mary Alice O'Brien, Russellville, Arkansas

SHRIMP A LA KING

1/4 c. chopped green pepper	1/2 c. milk
1 tbsp. butter	1 c. diced cooked shrimp
1 can frozen cream of shrimp	1 tbsp. chopped pimento
soup, thawed	4 patty shells

Cook the green pepper in butter in a saucepan until tender, then add the soup, milk, shrimp and pimento. Bring to a boil, then reduce heat and simmer until heated through, stirring occasionally. Serve in patty shells. 4 servings.

Mrs. P. J. Neils, Plantation, Florida

PINEAPPLE SHRIMP EN CROUSTADES

1/3 c. butter	1 tbsp. Worcestershire sauce
1 1/2 lb. cooked deveined	1 1/2 c. whipping cream
shrimp	1/2 c. sour cream
3 tbsp. cornstarch	1/4 c. dry sherry
1 tsp. salt	1 1-lb. 4 1/2-oz. can
Dash of hot sauce	pineapple chunks
1 tsp. paprika	Croustades or patty shells
1/2 tsp. monosodium glutamate	

Melt the butter in a skillet or chafing dish, then add the shrimp and stir until the shrimp are coated. Sprinkle with the cornstarch, stirring until well blended. Add the seasonings, then stir in the cream slowly. Heat, stirring until the mixture bubbles and thickens. Stir in the sour cream slowly, then add the sherry. Drain the pineapple and stir in the chunks gently. Heat thoroughly. Serve in croustades. 6-8 servings.

Photograph for this recipe on page 124.

CURRIED SHRIMP

3 tbsp. flour	1/4 tsp. ground ginger
1 tbsp. curry powder	3 tbsp. butter
1 tsp. salt	3 c. milk
1/2 c. sugar	3 c. boiled shrimp

Combine the flour, curry powder, salt, sugar and ginger. Melt the butter in the top of a double boiler, then stir in the flour mixture. Add the milk gradually, stirring constantly, and cook until the sauce is thick and smooth. Add the shrimp and cook until heated through, stirring frequently. Serve the shrimp over rice and top with chutney, grated coconut and crushed peanuts.

Mrs. Walter Cosby, Devereux, Georgia

SHRIMP ELEGANTE

2 tbsp. minced onion	3 tbsp. chili sauce
2 tbsp. butter	1 2/3 c. water
1 lb. fresh shrimp, cleaned	1 1/3 c. instant rice
1 med. can mushrooms	1 c. sour cream
1 tsp. salt	1 tbsp. flour
1/2 tsp. pepper	1 tbsp. chopped chives

Saute the onion in butter in a large skillet until golden brown. Add the shrimp and mushrooms and cook until the shrimp are pink, stirring constantly. Combine the salt, pepper, chili sauce and water and add to the shrimp mixture. Bring to a boil, then stir in rice. Cover and cook for 5 minutes. Combine the sour cream and flour and stir into the rice mixture. Cook until heated through, stirring carefully. Sprinkle each serving with chives. 4 servings.

Mrs. Herman Bunyard, Meridian, Mississippi

SHRIMP CREOLE

1/2 c. chopped onion	1 tsp. salt
1/2 c. sliced celery	1/8 tsp. pepper
1/2 c. chopped green pepper	1/4 tsp. chili pepper
1 clove of garlic, chopped	1 lb. cooked shrimp
1/4 c. pure vegetable oil	4 c. cooked rice
2 8-oz. cans tomato sauce	

Saute the onion, celery, green pepper and garlic in oil in large saucepan until golden, then add the tomato sauce and seasonings. Bring to a boil, then simmer for 15 minutes. Add the shrimp and heat thoroughly, stirring frequently. Serve over hot cooked rice. 4 servings.

Sharon Holmes, Clarendon, Arkansas

RICE RING WITH CURRIED SHRIMP

1 1/2 c. rice	1 c. chicken bouillon
3 tbsp. butter or margarine	1/2 c. cream
1 finely diced apple	1 1/2 lb. frozen cleaned
1/2 tsp. curry powder	shrimp
3 tbsp. flour	

Prepare the rice according to package directions. Melt the butter in a frypan and add the apple and curry powder, then fry until the apple is softened. Sprinkle with the flour and stir, then add the bouillon and cream. Cook over medium heat, stirring, until thickened. Drop the shrimp into boiling water and boil for 3 minutes, then drain. Pack the rice into a hot water-rinsed ring mold, then turn out on a hot serving dish. Stir the boiled shrimp into the curry sauce, then turn into the center of ring. Garnish with lettuce and fried banana slices.

Rice Ring with Curried Shrimp (above)

PATIO SHRIMP IN BEER

5 lb. shrimp	Pinch of cayenne pepper
6 cans beer	Tops of 8 green onions
4 tbsp. dry mustard	Leaves of 1 stalk celery
1 tbsp. salt	

Combine all the ingredients in a large kettle and bring to a boil, then simmer for about 5 minutes or until the shrimp turn pink. Let shrimp cool in the beer mixture, then drain and chill. Place in a large bowl to serve and let guests peel their own shrimp.

Mrs. Robert Vance, Biloxi, Mississippi

SHRIMP MARENGO

3 1/2 lb. shrimp	1 tsp. monosodium glutamate
7 slices bacon, diced	1 1/2 tsp. oregano
1 clove of garlic, crushed	1 tbsp. sugar
1 8-oz. can mushroom pieces, drained	1 1/2 tsp. sweet basil
1 med. onion, chopped	1 tbsp. salt
2 14-oz. cans Italian tomatoes	1/8 tsp. pepper
1 6-oz. can tomato paste	3 drops of hot sauce
1 10 1/2-oz. can consomme	2 tbsp. prepared mustard
	1/4 c. flour

Cook shrimp in large amount of boiling water for 7 minutes, then drain and cool. Shell and devein shrimp. Cook bacon in blazer pan of chafing dish over low heat until crisp. Remove bacon. Saute the garlic, mushrooms and onion in bacon drippings until onion is tender. Add tomatoes, tomato paste, shrimp, bacon, consomme, monosodium glutamate, oregano, sugar, sweet basil, salt, pepper, hot sauce and mustard and cook for 10 minutes, stirring frequently. Mix flour with 1/2 cup water until smooth and add to shrimp mixture, stirring constantly. Cook for about 1 minute longer. Keep hot over water until ready to serve. 10 servings.

Mrs. Susan Sockwell, Decatur, Georgia

POACHED BASS

1 bass	4 whole allspice
1/2 c. white vinegar	2 bay leaves
1 tsp. salt	3/4 c. melted butter
1 lge. onion, sliced	Juice of 1 lemon

Scale, draw and wash the bass. Place in large piece of cheesecloth. Place in a large pan, then add water to cover, vinegar, salt, onion, allspice and bay leaves. Simmer for 20 to 30 minutes or until done. Remove the bass from the cheesecloth and place on platter. Remove the skin and bone and cut into serving pieces. Combine the butter and lemon juice and pour over the bass. Garnish with parsley.

Mrs. Eva Walker, Pensacola, Florida

SMOKED HERRING

4 smoked herring	1/8 tsp. sugar
1/2 c. water	1/8 tsp. salt
2 tbsp. lemon juice	Dash of pepper

Remove heads from herring carefully and discard. Place herring in a skillet. Add the water, lemon juice, sugar, salt and pepper and cover. Cook over medium heat for 10 minutes or until herring are heated through and liquid has evaporated. Garnish with parsley, if desired. 4 servings.

Mrs. A. Vachon, Dallas, Texas

POACHED SALMON IMPERIAL

1 6-8 lb. whole dressed salmon	1/4 c. pickling spice
	3 lge. onions, sliced
3 qt. water	2 bay leaves
1 c. white vinegar	3 tbsp. salt
1/2 c. lemon juice	

Place the salmon on the greased flat tray of a poacher. Combine the water, vinegar, lemon juice, spice, onions, bay leaves and salt in the poacher, then bring to a boil and reduce the heat. Lower the salmon into liquid, being sure the salmon is covered with the liquid. Cover and simmer for 5 to 10 minutes per pound or just until fish flakes easily when tested with a fork. Remove the salmon carefully from the pan and cool slightly. Remove the skin and bones from fish. Chill overnight. Arrange on a platter and garnish with mayonnaise, capers, lemon-lime flowerettes, kumquat flowers and parsley. 8-10 servings.

Poached Salmon Imperial (above)

POACHED SALMON STEAKS

6 slices lemon	3 peppercorns
2 slices onion	4 salmon steaks, 1 in. thick
1 bay leaf	1 5-oz. jar hollandaise
Salt to taste	sauce

Fill a large frypan 1/2 full with water, then add 2 lemon slices, onion, bay leaf, salt and peppercorns. Bring to a boil. Place the salmon in the pan and cover. Simmer for 15 minutes or until fish flakes easily when tested with fork, then drain. Heat the hollandaise sauce according to package directions. Place the salmon on a platter, then spoon the sauce over the salmon. Garnish with the remaining lemon slices. 4 servings.

Mrs. Anita Lane, Spartanburg, South Carolina

SALMON POACHED IN COURT BOUILLON

1 lge. onion, sliced	2 bay leaves
4 carrots, sliced	1 bouquet garni
2 stalks celery, sliced	1 6-lb. whole salmon

Combine 2 quarts water, onion, carrots, celery, bay leaves and bouquet garni in a large kettle, then bring to a boil and skim. Reduce the heat and simmer for 30 minutes. Cool slightly. Wrap salmon in cheesecloth and lower into the bouillon, adding water if needed to cover. Simmer for 45 minutes to 1 hour or until fish flakes easily with a fork. Remove the salmon carefully from the liquid and unwrap. Remove the skin carefully and arrange on a hot platter. Garnish with lemon slices, cucumber, watercress or parsley.

Sauce

1 c. mayonnaise	2 tbsp. lemon juice
2 tbsp. minced watercress	Freshly ground pepper to
2 tbsp. minced tarragon	taste
leaves	Salt to taste
2 tbsp. minced onion	

Combine all the ingredients and mix well. Serve with the salmon.

Mrs. Joyce Black, Austin, Texas

HALIBUT STEAK WITH ORANGE-GRAPE SAUCE

2 halibut steaks, 3/4 in.	1 tsp. salt
thick	1 tbsp. cornstarch
2 c. boiling water	1 tbsp. sugar
2 tbsp. lemon juice	1/2 c. orange juice

1/2 c. cold water	1 11-oz. can mandarin orange
2 tsp. grated orange rind	segments, drained
1 tsp. lemon juice	1 c. seeded green grape halves

Place the fish in a well-greased, large frypan, then add the boiling water, lemon juice and salt. Cover and simmer for 8 to 10 minutes or until fish flakes easily when tested with a fork. Combine the cornstarch and sugar in a small saucepan, then stir in the orange juice and cold water. Simmer, stirring constantly, until thickened. Stir in the orange rind, lemon juice and fruits and heat through. Drain the fish and place carefully on a hot serving platter. Spoon sauce over halibut. Garnish with orange slices and mint. 6 servings.

GREEN PEPPER FISH

3 onions	1 pkg. frozen cod fillets
1 green pepper	1 tsp. salt
5 tbsp. butter	Dash of white pepper
1 leek, chopped	

Peel the onions and cut into slices. Remove the seeds from the green pepper, then cut into strips. Melt the butter in a heavy saucepan. Saute the onions and leek until limp. Place the fillets in the saucepan. Season with the salt and pepper and cover with the green pepper. Add 1 cup water, then cover. Simmer for about 20 minutes. Remove the fillets and vegetables carefully from the saucepan and place in a serving dish. Pour liquid from saucepan over the fillets and vegetables.

Green Pepper Fish (above)

POACHED SALMON STEAKS WITH EGG SAUCE

2 1/2 tbsp. butter	Celery leaves to taste
2 1/2 tbsp. flour	1 bay leaf
1 1/2 c. milk	1 lemon slice
1 tsp. salt	1 onion slice
1/8 tsp. pepper	4 fresh salmon steaks
2 hard-cooked eggs, chopped	3 c. cooked green peas

Melt the butter in heavy saucepan, then stir in the flour. Remove from the heat and stir in the milk slowly. Cook until thickened, stirring constantly. Add the salt, pepper and eggs. Place the celery leaves, bay leaf, lemon and onion in a large skillet with 1 1/2 inches boiling salted water and boil for 3 minutes. Add the salmon and cover, then reduce the heat. Simmer for about 6 minutes. Remove the salmon to a platter and pour the egg mixture over the salmon. Spoon the peas around the salmon. 4 servings.

Mrs. Lillian Herman, Bay City, Texas

FILLET OF SOLE WITH WHITE GRAPES

1/4 c. butter or margarine	3 peppercorns
3 green onions, chopped	Pinch of nutmeg
8 sole fillets	1 1/4 c. milk
Salt and pepper to taste	2 tbsp. flour
1 c. white wine	1 egg yolk, beaten
1 c. water	1 c. seedless white grapes
1 bay leaf	1/2 c. whipped cream

Melt half the butter in a frypan and sprinkle with green onions. Season the fillets with salt and pepper and fold in half. Arrange over the green onions. Pour the wine and water over the fillets. Cut a piece of greased paper 1 inch larger than the frypan and cut a small hole in center. Place over the frypan. Bring to a boil and reduce heat. Simmer for 10 to 15 minutes. Remove the fillets and place in an ovenproof dish. Keep warm. Add the bay leaf, peppercorns, nutmeg and milk to the frypan and simmer until liquid is reduced to 1 1/4 cups. Strain the liquid. Melt remaining butter in a saucepan. Stir in the flour and cook for 1 minute. Add the strained liquid gradually and cook, stirring constantly, until thickened. Cool slightly. Stir in the egg yolk. Simmer the grapes in a small amount of water for 2 minutes, then drain. Place around the fillets. Fold whipped cream into the sauce and reheat. Do not boil. Pour over fillets.

Mrs. L. M. Moore, San Angelo, Texas

POACHED TROUT

Celery leaves to taste	Grated rind of 1/2 lemon
1 sprig of parsley	Juice of 1/2 lemon
1 tsp. salt	1 fresh trout, cleaned
6 peppercorns	

Place enough water in a skillet to cover the trout. Add the celery leaves, parsley, salt, peppercorns, rind and juice and bring to a boil. Add the trout carefully and simmer until the trout flakes easily when tested with a fork. Drain and serve at once.

Mrs. B. A. Emerson, Greenville, South Carolina

POACHED FISH WITH EGG SAUCE

2 lb. fish fillets	1 tsp. salt
2 c. boiling water	3 peppercorns
1/4 c. lemon juice	2 sprigs of parsley
1 sm. onion, thinly sliced	1 bay leaf

Remove any skin and bones from the fish, then place in a well-greased 10-inch frypan. Add the remaining ingredients, then cover and simmer for 5 to 10 minutes or until fish flakes easily when tested with a fork. Remove the fish carefully to a hot platter.

Egg Sauce

1/4 c. butter or margarine	Dash of pepper
2 tbsp. flour	1 1/4 c. milk
3/4 tsp. powdered mustard	2 hard-cooked eggs, chopped
1/2 tsp. salt	1 tbsp. chopped parsley

Melt the butter in a saucepan, then stir in the flour and seasonings. Add the milk gradually and cook until thick and smooth, stirring constantly. Add the eggs and parsley, and heat through. May pour the sauce over the fish to serve or serve sauce separately.

Poached Fish with Egg Sauce (above)

Clam and Spaghetti Casserole (page 142)

seafood casseroles

Casseroles are distinguished and flavorful standby foods that are prized by homemakers for their convenience of serving. And seafood casseroles are the most appreciated of all because they provide menu variety for you and your family. But a welcome change from the routine meat-and-potatoes meal is not the whole story. Seafood casseroles are also quickly and easily prepared, often from canned or frozen ingredients that you are likely to have on hand.

Seafood casseroles *are* so distinctive because any number of diverse ingredients merge so deliciously. Fish and shellfish combinations such as Salmon-Oyster Casserole and Elegant Seafood Casserole are two such appetizing mixtures. But you will also be delighted with the selection of seafood-vegetable combinations. Fillets Divan with broccoli, Crab-Zucchini Casserole, and Eggplant Shrimp Casserole are some of the luscious examples.

Other ingredients that appear with regularity on your kitchen shelf are pasta and rice; and in your refrigerator, cheese. Here you have the makings for tasty seafood casseroles like Tuna Romanoff, Lobster-Noodle Casserole, and Rice and Salmon Casserole. These foods are valued particularly for their mild, almost bland flavor that does not overwhelm the excellent taste of fish or shellfish. For unbeatable seafood casseroles, you can rely on them often.

ALBACORE CASSEROLE

2 tsp. chopped parsley	1 c. slivered almonds
2 sm. onions, chopped	4 cans cream of chicken soup
4 c. chopped celery	4 6 1/4-oz. cans albacore
Butter	1 lge. can evaporated milk
2 c. water	Buttered crumbs
1 pkg. herb-seasoned stuffing mix	

Saute the parsley, onions and celery in small amount of butter until soft, then stir in the water and stuffing mix and mix well. Place in a greased 13 x 9-inch baking dish. Sprinkle 1/2 cup almonds over dressing and add 2 cans soup. Add the albacore in an even layer and pour in remaining soup. Pour milk over the soup and top with buttered crumbs and remaining almonds. Bake for 30 minutes in 375-degree oven. 16 servings.

Mrs. Mary F. Clark, Raleigh, North Carolina

CLAM AND SPAGHETTI CASSEROLE

2 tbsp. flour	1/4 c. milk
Dash of pepper	2 7-oz. cans minced clams
4 tbsp. melted margarine	1 8-oz. package spaghetti
1 can mushroom soup	1/2 c. dry bread crumbs

Blend the flour and pepper with 2 tablespoons melted margarine in a saucepan, then add the soup, milk, and clams. Cook, stirring constantly, until thick. Cook the spaghetti according to package directions and drain. Combine with the clam sauce, then turn into a well-greased 1 1/2-quart casserole. Combine the remaining melted margarine with the bread crumbs, then sprinkle over the casserole. Bake at 400 degrees for 10 minutes or until crumbs are lightly browned. 6 servings.

Photograph for this recipe on page 140.

CLAM CASSEROLE

2 eggs, beaten slightly	1/4 c. melted butter
1 8-oz. can minced clams	24 soda crackers, crushed
1 c. milk	

Mix the eggs, clams and liquid, milk, butter and cracker crumbs and place in a greased baking dish. Bake at 325 degrees for 45 minutes to 1 hour.

Mary E. Stanton, Chelsea, Oklahoma

BAKED WILD RICE AND SEAFOOD

2 c. cooked wild rice	1 sm. can pimento strips, drained
1 c. cooked rice	3 cans mushroom soup
1 c. flaked crab meat	1 c. chopped shrimp
1 1/2 c. chopped celery	1 lb. mushrooms, sliced
1 green pepper, chopped	Butter
1 med. onion, chopped	

Combine the first 7 ingredients, then add 1 1/2 cans soup and 1/2 cup shrimp and mix well. Place in a baking dish. Bake at 350 degrees for 45 minutes. Brown the mushrooms in a small amount of butter in a skillet. Add remaining soup and shrimp and heat through. Serve crab meat mixture with the mushroom sauce. 20 servings.

Mrs. Phil Turnipseed, Louisville, Kentucky

PAELLA

4 tbsp. olive oil	1 can mushrooms
1 broiler-fryer chicken, disjointed	1 1-lb. can peas
1 tsp. monosodium glutamate	1 can bouillon
2 tsp. salt	1/2 tsp. saffron
1 c. diced celery	1/4 tsp. hot sauce
1/2 c. chopped onion	1 lb. cooked shrimp
2 c. diced ham	1 1/2 lb. mussels or clams
	1 13-oz. box instant rice

Pour the olive oil in a large skillet or deep kettle and heat. Sprinkle the chicken with the monosodium glutamate and half the salt. Brown the chicken in the oil, then add the celery and onion and cook for about 5 minutes. Add the ham. Drain the mushrooms and add the liquid to skillet, then cover tightly and cook over low heat for about 30 minutes. Drain the liquid from the peas into a 1-quart measure, then add the bouillon and enough water to make 4 cups. Add the remaining salt, saffron and hot sauce. Pour into the skillet and add the shrimp, peas and mussels. Bring to a boil, then sprinkle the rice into the hot mixture. Toss until the rice is dampened, then simmer for 5 minutes. Turn into an ovenproof dish. Bake at 350 degrees for 10 to 15 minutes or until lightly browned. 8 servings.

Paella (above)

143

ELEGANT SEAFOOD CASSEROLE

2 slices bread, cubed	1/2 tsp. curry powder
2 cans crab meat	1 tbsp. dry mustard
2 cans shrimp, drained	1 tsp. Worcestershire sauce
1/2 c. chopped onion	1 tsp. minced capers
1/2 c. chopped celery	1/4 c. cooking sherry
1 tbsp. chopped parsley	1 c. mayonnaise
1 tsp. salt	2/3 c. water

Place the bread cubes in a buttered casserole and cover with the crab and shrimp. Saute the onion, celery and parsley in a small amount of fat in a skillet until soft. Combine the sauteed vegetables and remaining ingredients in a bowl and mix well, then pour over the crab and shrimp. Bake at 325 degrees for 30 minutes and serve hot.

Mrs. L. P. Enzor, Nichols, South Carolina

FILLET OF SOLE NEWBURG

1 pkg. frozen sole fillets	5 c. bread cubes
1 pkg. frozen lobster Newburg	3 tbsp. melted butter
1 tsp. dried onion flakes	Salt and pepper to taste
1 tsp. dried pepper flakes	1 tbsp. olive oil

Thaw the sole fillets and lobster Newburg partially. Soak the onion flakes and pepper flakes in 1/4 cup water in a large bowl. Add the bread, butter, salt and pepper and mix well. Grease a 2-quart casserole with the oil and arrange sole in the casserole. Spread with the bread mixture and top with the lobster Newburg. Bake at 350 degrees for about 40 minutes. 6 servings.

Elizabeth H. Corley, New Orleans, Louisiana

SALMON-OYSTER CASSEROLE

1 lge. can salmon, drained	Salt and pepper to taste
1 can oysters, drained	Dash of monosodium glutamate
1 c. milk	2 c. cracker crumbs
1 med. onion, chopped	Butter
2 eggs, well beaten	

Combine all the ingredients except butter in a casserole and mix well, then dot with butter. Bake at 350 degrees for 45 to 60 minutes or until brown.

Mrs. Beatrice Kohler, Bentonville, Arkansas

MIXED SEAFOOD CASSEROLE

1 lb. med. shrimp	1 lb. sole fillets
Salt	3/4 c. butter
1 lb. scallops	3 tbsp. flour

3 tall cans evaporated milk | Grated Parmesan cheese
2 tbsp. sherry | 1 tsp. paprika
1 tbsp. Worcestershire sauce | 1/2 lb. crab meat, flaked
1 tbsp. chopped capers | 1/2 c. dry bread crumbs

Shell and devein the shrimp. Bring 2 quarts water and 2 tablespoons salt to a boil in a large saucepan, then add the shrimp and scallops and cook for 2 minutes. Add the sole and cook for 3 minutes longer. Chop the scallops and flake the sole. Melt the butter in a saucepan and blend in the flour. Add the milk gradually and cook over low heat, stirring constantly, until thick. Add the sherry, Worcestershire sauce, capers, 2 tablespoons Parmesan cheese, 1 1/2 teaspoons salt and the paprika. Fold in the shrimp, scallops, sole and crab meat. Pour into a 3-quart casserole. Mix 1/4 cup Parmesan cheese and the bread crumbs in a bowl and sprinkle over casserole. Bake at 350 degrees for 40 minutes. 8-10 servings.

Mrs. I. C. O'Brien, St Petersburg, Florida

PARTY SEAFOOD

4 c. cooked peeled shrimp | 2 tsp. Worcestershire sauce
1 7-oz. can lobster | 1 tsp. salt
1 7 1/2-oz. can crab meat | 1/2 tsp. pepper
2 1/2 c. thinly sliced celery | 1 1/2 c. fine dry bread crumbs
2/3 c. finely chopped onion | 1/3 c. margarine, melted
1 c. mayonnaise

Cut shrimp into halves, lengthwise, then flake the lobster and crab meat. Combine the seafood, then mix in the celery, onion, mayonnaise, Worcestershire sauce, salt and pepper. Place in a 1 1/2-quart casserole. Combine the bread crumbs and margarine and sprinkle over the casserole. Bake at 350 degrees for 30 to 35 minutes or until lightly browned. Garnish with lemon slices and parsley. 6-8 servings.

Party Seafood (above)

SEAFOOD-NUT CASSEROLE

1 sm. can crab meat	1/4 c. chopped pimento
1 sm. can shrimp, drained	2 tbsp. chopped green pepper
1 can mushroom or celery soup	Dash of pepper
1 c. cashews	1/2 c. corn flake crumbs
1/2 c. chopped celery	

Combine all the ingredients except corn flake crumbs in a bowl and mix well. Pour into a greased round baking dish and top with corn flake crumbs. Bake at 350 degrees for 25 to 30 minutes. 5-6 servings.

Mrs. George L. Orth, El Paso, Texas

BOUNTIFUL SEASIDE CASSEROLE

1 loaf day-old bread	1/2 lb. cooked lobster meat
4 c. milk	2 hard-cooked eggs, sliced
1 tbsp. melted butter	1/2 lb. grated mozzarella
1 tsp. salt	cheese
1/8 tsp. pepper	Paprika to taste
1/2 lb. cooked crab meat	1/2 c. dry bread crumbs
1 lb. flaked cooked halibut	1/2 bay leaf

Cut the bread in cubes and place in a large bowl. Pour the milk over the bread and let stand for 30 minutes. Stir in the butter, salt and pepper. Stir in the crab meat, halibut and lobster gently. Pour the seafood into a large, buttered shallow pan and cover with the eggs. Sprinkle with the cheese, paprika and bread crumbs. Place the bay leaf in the center and push into the seafood mixture. Bake at 400 degrees for about 20 minutes or until brown and bubbly.

Margery E. Carlson, Baltimore, Maryland

Company Crab Casseroles (page 147)

ARTICHOKE-CRAB MEAT CASSEROLE

4 tbsp. margarine	1 1-lb. can artichoke
4 tbsp. flour	hearts, drained
1/8 tsp. salt	2 cans crab meat
1/8 tsp. pepper	4 hard-boiled eggs, quartered
2 c. milk	1/2 c. grated Parmesan cheese

Melt the margarine in a saucepan, then blend in the flour, salt and pepper. Add the milk gradually. Cook and stir until the sauce is thick. Remove from heat and stir in the artichoke hearts, crab meat and eggs. Place in a 1 1/2-quart casserole and sprinkle with the cheese. Bake in 350-degree oven for 30 minutes. 6 servings.

Mrs. Laura Martin, Birmingham, Alabama

ASPARAGUS-CRAB MEAT CASSEROLE

2 tbsp. butter or margarine	1 tsp. salt
2 tbsp. flour	1/8 tsp. pepper
1 2/3 c. milk	24 cooked asparagus spears
1/4 c. grated sharp Cheddar	1/2 lb. claw crab meat
cheese	Grated Parmesan cheese
1/4 c. grated Swiss cheese	

Melt the butter in a saucepan and stir in flour. Add the milk gradually and cook, stirring, until thick and smooth. Add the Cheddar and Swiss cheeses and stir until melted. Add seasonings. Place the asparagus in a 2-quart casserole. Place the crab meat over asparagus and cover with cheese sauce. Cover with Parmesan cheese. Bake in 375-degree oven for about 30 minutes. 8 servings.

Mrs. James L. Glymp, Baltimore, Maryland

COMPANY CRAB CASSEROLES

1 1-lb. can cut Blue Lake	1/2 tsp. lemon juice
green beans	1/4 tsp. crushed basil
1 can frozen cream of shrimp	1/4 tsp. crushed tarragon
soup	3/4 c. fine soft bread crumbs
1 7 1/2-oz. can crab meat	2 tbsp. butter, melted
1/4 c. finely chopped celery	2 tbsp. grated Parmesan cheese
2 tbsp. sherry	

Drain the green beans and reserve 1/4 cup liquid. Combine the liquid and soup in a saucepan and heat, stirring, until the soup thaws. Rinse, drain and flake the crab meat, then add to the soup mixture. Add the beans, celery, sherry, lemon juice and herbs and stir until mixed. Turn into 4 or 5 lightly buttered individual casseroles. Toss the bread crumbs in butter, then sprinkle around the edge of casseroles. Sprinkle the cheese over the top. Bake at 350 degrees for 20 minutes. 4-5 servings.

BAKED CRAB IMPERIAL

2 tsp. Worcestershire sauce	1 c. thick cream sauce
1/4 tsp. pepper	1 lb. crab meat
1 tsp. lemon juice	1 c. moist bread crumbs
1 tbsp. grated onion	1 c. diced sweet red pepper
1/2 tsp. dry mustard	1 c. fine dry bread crumbs
1/2 tsp. salt	Butter

Combine the Worcestershire sauce, pepper, lemon juice, onion, mustard, salt and cream sauce in a bowl and add the crab meat, moist bread crumbs and red pepper. Mix well and place in buttered ramekins or casserole. Sprinkle with dry bread crumbs and dot with butter. Bake at 425 degrees for 15 to 20 minutes.

Mrs. John Wilder, Auburn, Alabama

CRAB MEAT COBBLER

1/2 c. butter	1 c. shredded American cheese
1/2 c. chopped onions	1 c. cooked crab meat
1/2 c. chopped green pepper	1 1/2 c. drained tomatoes
1/2 c. flour	2 tsp. Worcestershire sauce
1 tsp. dry mustard	1/2 tsp. salt
1 c. milk	

Melt the butter in the top of a double boiler, then add the onions and green pepper and cook for 10 minutes or until tender. Blend in the flour and mustard. Stir in the milk gradually and cook over boiling water, stirring frequently, until thick. Add the cheese and stir until melted. Add the crab meat, tomatoes, Worcestershire sauce and salt and mix well. Turn into a 2-quart casserole.

Cheese Biscuit Topping

1 c. flour	1/4 c. shredded cheese
2 tsp. baking powder	2 tbsp. shortening
1/2 tsp. salt	1/2 c. milk

Sift the flour, baking powder and salt together into a bowl and add cheese. Cut in the shortening until mixture resembles fine meal. Add the milk and mix just until moistened. Drop by rounded teaspoonfuls on crab meat mixture. Bake at 425 degrees for 20 to 25 minutes or until biscuits are brown.

Mrs. Walter E. Douty, Abilene, Texas

CRAB AND HOMINY CASSEROLE

1 No. 2 can hominy, drained	1 c. grated American cheese
1 6 1/2-oz. can crab meat	1/2 c. bread crumbs
2 c. thin white sauce	

Grind the hominy in a food chopper with medium blade. Flake the crab meat. Place a layer of hominy in a greased 1 1/2-quart casserole and a layer of crab meat. Cover with half the white sauce and sprinkle with 1/2 cup cheese. Repeat layers. Top with bread crumbs and cover. Bake in 350-degree oven for 30 minutes. Remove cover and bake for 15 minutes longer. 6 servings.

Anna Lee Vaughn, Nashville, Tennessee

CRAB MEAT ST. JACQUES

1 sm. onion, chopped	Paprika
1 sm. green pepper, chopped	1 tsp. Worcestershire sauce
1/2 c. minced mushrooms	1 lb. cooked crab meat
Butter	1/4 c. grated American cheese
2 c. white sauce	1/4 c. buttered bread crumbs
Salt and pepper to taste	

Saute the onion, green pepper and mushrooms in a small amount of butter in a saucepan until onion is tender. Combine the white sauce, salt, pepper, a generous amount of paprika and Worcestershire sauce in another saucepan, then add to the mushroom mixture. Add the crab meat and stir until mixed. Turn into a buttered casserole and sprinkle with cheese, bread crumbs and paprika. Bake at 450 degrees for 15 minutes.

Mrs. John A. Bracey, Springfield, Tennessee

CRAB AND MUSHROOM CASSEROLE

1 lb. sliced mushrooms	Salt and pepper to taste
Butter	2 cans crab meat
Flour	1/2 c. buttered bread crumbs
1 10-oz. can chicken broth	1/2 c. grated American cheese
1 1/2 c. light cream	

Saute the mushrooms in 2 tablespoons butter in a saucepan for 5 minutes. Melt 6 tablespoons butter in a saucepan and blend in 1/3 cup flour. Add the chicken broth, cream, salt and pepper and cook, stirring, until thickened. Arrange alternate layers of mushrooms, sauce and crab meat in a 6-cup casserole and sprinkle with crumbs and cheese. Bake at 350 degrees for 30 minutes. 6 servings.

Alice Mays, Rockville, Maryland

SPECIAL CRAB CASSEROLE

1 7 1/2-oz. can crab meat	6 hard-boiled eggs, chopped
1 c. soft bread crumbs	Dash of salt and pepper
1 c. mayonnaise	Buttered bread crumbs
3/4 c. milk	

Drain the crab meat and place in a large bowl. Add the soft bread crumbs, mayonnaise, milk, eggs, salt and pepper and mix well. Place in a buttered 1-quart casserole and cover with the buttered crumbs. Bake at 350 degrees for 25 minutes or until brown. 6 servings.

Mrs. Roberta Williams, Wilmington, Delaware

DEVILED CRAB AND CORN CASSEROLE

4 tbsp. butter	1 c. crab meat
2 tbsp. flour	2 hard-boiled eggs, minced
1 tsp. prepared mustard	1 can whole kernel corn, drained
1/2 tsp. Worcestershire sauce	Salt and pepper to taste
1 tsp. horseradish	1/2 c. soft buttered bread
1 tbsp. lemon juice	crumbs
1 c. milk	1/2 c. grated Parmesan cheese

Melt the butter in a saucepan, then blend in the flour, mustard, Worcestershire sauce, horseradish and lemon juice. Add the milk gradually and cook, stirring constantly, until thickened. Add the crab meat, eggs, corn, salt and pepper and mix well, then turn into a buttered casserole. Top with the bread crumbs and cheese. Bake at 400 degrees for 15 minutes or until lightly browned.

Mrs. Ralph Fulkerson, Wichita Falls, Texas

CRAB-ZUCCHINI CASSEROLE

2 med. zucchini	1/2 lb. Swiss cheese
1 med. onion, chopped	3 tomatoes, coarsely chopped
1/2 c. butter	1 tsp. dried basil
2 cloves of garlic, crushed	Salt and pepper to taste
2 7 1/2-oz. cans crab meat	1 c. bread crumbs

Cut the zucchini in 1/4-inch thick slices. Saute the zucchini and onion in the butter in a saucepan until tender-crisp. Add the garlic and crab meat and mix lightly. Cut the Swiss cheese in strips. Add 1 cup cheese, tomatoes, basil, salt, pepper and 2/3 cup crumbs to the crab meat mixture and mix well. Turn into a casserole and cover with remaining cheese and crumbs. Bake at 375 degrees for 30 to 40 minutes. 6 servings.

Louise McRae Gaut, Oklahoma City, Oklahoma

CRAB MEAT AU GRATIN

1 sm. green pepper, minced	2 c. crab meat
1 sm. onion, chopped	1/2 tsp. salt
3 tbsp. butter	Dash of nutmeg
3 tbsp. flour	1/2 c. grated cheese
2 c. milk	1/2 c. buttered bread crumbs

Cook the green pepper and onion in butter in a saucepan for 5 minutes, then blend in the flour. Add the milk gradually and cook, stirring constantly, until thickened. Stir in the crab meat, salt and nutmeg, then pour into a greased, shallow baking dish or crab shells. Sprinkle with cheese and bread crumbs. Bake at 350 degrees until brown.

Mrs. E. H. Denton, Denison, Texas

DEVILED CRAB CASSEROLE

1 lb. lump crab meat	Celery salt to taste
2 tbsp. applesauce	Pepper to taste
3 tbsp. mayonnaise	Paprika to taste
1 tbsp. minced onion	Dash of monosodium glutamate
1 tbsp. minced parsley	2 slices Swiss cheese
2 tbsp. lemon juice	1/2 c. buttered bread crumbs

Combine the first 6 ingredients in a large bowl, then add the celery salt, pepper, paprika and monosodium glutamate. Mix lightly and turn into a casserole. Cut the cheese in small pieces and mix with the bread crumbs. Sprinkle over the crab meat mixture. Bake at 350 degrees for 20 to 25 minutes. 4 servings.

Mrs. R. E. Davis, Groves, Texas

ONE-DISH FISH DINNER

1 lb. frozen fish fillets	1/4 tsp. pepper
1 stick margarine	2/3 c. evaporated milk
1/4 c. minced onion	2 med. potatoes, cooked
1/2 c. flour	1 10-oz. package frozen peas
1/2 c. corn flake crumbs	and carrots
1 tsp. salt	

Thaw the fish fillets at room temperature. Melt the margarine in a saucepan and add the onion. Saute until tender and set aside. Place the flour, crumbs, salt and pepper in a paper bag and mix well. Wash and dry the fish. Dip the fish in milk in a shallow dish, then shake with corn flake mixture in the bag until thoroughly coated. Arrange the fish in the center of a baking dish. Slice the potatoes around the fish, then pour the onion mixture over top. Bake in 375-degree oven for 20 to 25 minutes. Broil until the fish is brown. Cook the peas and carrots according to package directions and drain. Spoon over the potatoes. 4 servings.

Mrs. Phyllis Gardner, Albuquerque, New Mexico

ELEGANT FLOUNDER SUPREME

2 lb. frozen flounder fillets	1 1/2 c. cooked rice
1 1/4 tsp. salt	1/2 c. blanched slivered
Pepper to taste	almonds, toasted
1 can cream of shrimp soup	1/4 c. chopped parsley
3/4 c. sour cream	Paprika to taste
Dash of nutmeg	

Thaw the flounder and cut into serving portions and sprinkle with 1 teaspoon salt and pepper. Combine the soup, sour cream and nutmeg in a bowl and reserve 3/4 cup soup mixture. Combine remaining soup mixture with the rice, 1/4 cup almonds, parsley, remaining salt and pepper. Spread in a well-greased baking dish and place the flounder over the rice mixture. Spread reserved soup mixture over the flounder and sprinkle with remaining almonds and paprika. Bake at 350 degrees for 35 to 40 minutes. 6 servings.

Mrs. Bennett Moore, Eupora, Mississippi

Cucumber-Flounder Rolls with Shrimp-Cucumber Sauce (below)

CUCUMBER-FLOUNDER ROLLS WITH SHRIMP-CUCUMBER SAUCE

4 cucumbers	1 1/2 c. soft bread crumbs
2 tbsp. wine vinegar	1/4 c. chopped fresh parsley
1 tsp. salt	1 tsp. snipped fresh dill
1/8 tsp. sugar	1 tbsp. fresh lemon juice
2 tbsp. butter or margarine	6 lge. flounder fillets
3 tbsp. chopped fresh onion	Shrimp-Cucumber Sauce

Pare the cucumbers and cut in half lengthwise, then scoop out the seeds with a spoon. Cut into cubes. Mix the vinegar, salt and sugar together in a large bowl, then add the cucumbers and mix well. Marinate at room temperature for 30 minutes. Drain and pat dry. Reserve 1 1/2 cups cucumbers for sauce. Melt the butter in a large skillet, then add the onion and cook until tender. Add the bread crumbs, parsley, dill and lemon juice and simmer for 10 minutes. Add the remaining cucumbers to stuffing mixture and cook slowly for 5 minutes. Place 1/4 cup of the stuffing on each fillet and roll up, securing ends with food picks. Place in shallow 1 1/2-quart casserole and pour Shrimp-Cucumber Sauce over top. Bake, uncovered, in 325-degree oven for 20 to 30 minutes. Garnish with cucumber slices and fresh dill.

Shrimp-Cucumber Sauce

3 tbsp. butter or margarine	3 tbsp. white wine
2 tbsp. chopped fresh onion	1/4 c. snipped fresh dill
1/4 c. flour	1/4 tsp. salt
2 c. milk	1/2 lb. cleaned shrimp

Melt the butter in a large saucepan, then add the onion and cook until tender. Blend in flour and stir in the milk. Cook, stirring constantly, until mixture thickens and comes to a boil. Stir in the wine, reserved cucumber, dill, salt and shrimp. Simmer for 5 minutes.

FILLETS DIVAN

1 1-lb. package frozen fish fillets	1/2 c. mayonnaise
1 pkg. frozen broccoli	1/4 c. finely chopped parsley
1/2 c. grated American cheese	3 tbsp. pickle relish
Salt	1 tbsp. lemon juice
1/2 tsp. pepper	1 tsp. minced onion
	2 egg whites

Thaw the fish fillets. Cook the broccoli according to package directions and drain, then arrange in a single layer in a 9-inch square baking dish. Place the fillets in a single layer over the broccoli. Sprinkle the cheese, 1/2 teaspoon salt and pepper over the fillets. Combine the mayonnaise, parsley, relish, lemon juice, onion and salt to taste in a small bowl. Beat the egg whites until stiff peaks form, then fold into the mayonnaise mixture. Spread over the fillets. Bake in a 400-degree oven for 30 minutes or until fillets are done and the sauce is puffy and golden. 4 servings.

Mrs. Henry Sherrer, Bay City, Texas

RICH LOBSTER CASSEROLE

2 9-oz. packages frozen artichokes	3 5-oz. cans lobster
Seasoned salt to taste	2 cans cream of mushroom soup
2 4 1/2-oz. packages precooked rice	2 soup cans water
	Sliced American process cheese
	Chopped parsley or chives

Cook the artichokes according to package directions and drain. Place in a 3-quart casserole and sprinkle with seasoned salt and rice. Drain the lobster and place over the rice. Blend the mushroom soup and water and pour over the lobster. Bake at 400 degrees for 40 minutes or until the sauce is bubbly. Cut slices of cheese in half to form triangles, then arrange over the casserole. Sprinkle with parsley.

Mrs. Raymond Miles, Headland, Alabama

FISH AND NOODLES

3 tbsp. chopped onion	1 2/3 c. canned tomatoes
1/3 c. diced celery	1 2/3 c. cooked noodles
1 tbsp. cooking oil	2 c. flaked cooked fish
1/2 tsp. salt	Buttered crumbs
Pepper to taste	

Cook the onion and celery in oil in a saucepan until tender. Add the salt, pepper and tomatoes and bring to a boil. Place alternate layers of noodles, fish and tomato mixture in a greased baking dish and cover with crumbs. Bake at 350 degrees for 30 minutes or until heated through and crumbs are browned.

Mrs. Charles H. Anderson, Manor, Texas

LOBSTER-NOODLE CASSEROLE

10 rock lobster-tails	4 c. milk
1/2 c. butter	1 c. cream
1/4 c. flour	1/2 c. dry sherry
2 1/2 tsp. salt	1 12-oz. package broad
1 1/2 tsp. paprika	noodles
1/2 tsp. pepper	Buttered bread crumbs
1 tsp. instant minced onion	1/4 c. capers, drained
1 tsp. angostura bitters	

Cook the lobster-tails according to package directions. Slice each in half length-wise and remove lobster meat from shells. Cut half the lobster into chunks. Melt 1/4 cup butter in a saucepan and stir in the flour, salt, paprika, pepper, onion and bitters. Add milk and cream and cook until thickened, stirring constantly. Add the sherry and lobster chunks. Cook the noodles according to package directions and stir in the lobster mixture. Place in 3-quart casserole and cover with buttered bread crumbs. Bake at 375 degrees for about 30 minutes or until bubbly. Top with lobster halves in pinwheel design. Melt remaining butter and stir in the capers. Pour over lobster halves and bake for 10 minutes longer. 6-8 servings.

Mrs. Chris Sterling, Oklahoma City, Oklahoma

OYSTER CASSEROLE

2 c. cracker crumbs	2 tsp. minced parsley
1 tbsp. chopped pimento	1/2 c. melted butter
1 tsp. salt	1 pt. oysters, drained
1/4 tsp. paprika	1 egg, slightly beaten
1/4 tsp. celery salt	2/3 c. cream of mushroom soup

Combine the crumbs, pimento, salt, paprika, celery salt, parsley and butter and mix well. Line a shallow casserole with half the crumb mixture. Combine the oysters, egg and soup and pour over the crumb mixture. Cover with remaining crumb mixture. Bake at 350 degrees for 45 minutes.

Mrs. A. M. Tennison, Nashville, Tennessee

OYSTER PUDDING

2 pt. oysters	1 c. melted butter
1 tsp. salt	4 c. cracker crumbs
Pepper to taste	1 1/2 c. cream
1 tsp. Worcestershire sauce	

Drain the oysters, reserving liquid. Combine the salt, pepper, Worcestershire sauce, butter and crumbs. Place alternate layers of crumb mixture and oysters in a casserole. Combine 1 cup reserved oyster liquid and cream and pour over casserole. Bake in 350-degree oven for 45 minutes or until done.

Mrs. Russell Ivan, Horatio, Arkansas

SCALLOPED OYSTERS DELUXE

1 pt. oysters	Paprika to taste
Butter	1/2 c. heavy cream
1/4 lb. saltines, crushed	1 tbsp. Worcestershire sauce
3 tbsp. minced shallots	4 drops of hot sauce
Salt and pepper to taste	1/4 c. dry white wine

Drain the oysters and reserve 1/2 cup liquor. Butter a casserole generously. Place 1/4 of the saltines in the casserole. Cover with 1/3 of the oysters and sprinkle with 1/3 of the shallots. Sprinkle with salt, pepper and paprika and dot with butter. Repeat layers twice, then sprinkle with remaining saltines. Dot with butter. Combine reserved oyster liquor with the cream, Worcestershire sauce, hot sauce and wine and pour over the casserole. Bake in 400-degree oven for 30 minutes. 6 servings.

Mrs. R. L. Knight, Florence, Alabama

FILLET OF SOLE PANE

1 4 1/2-oz. jar sliced mushrooms, drained	Pepper to taste
3 tbsp. butter, melted	1 1/2 lb. sole fillets
1/2 c. chopped pecans	1 egg, well beaten
Salt	1/4 c. milk
	3/4 c. fine bread crumbs

Preheat oven to 400 degrees. Saute the mushrooms in the butter until lightly browned. Stir in the pecans and sprinkle lightly with salt and pepper. Spread the pecan mixture on the fillets. Roll tightly and skewer with toothpicks. Combine the egg, milk and 1/2 teaspoon salt. Dip the fillets in the egg mixture, then roll in the crumbs. Place in a well-greased 8-inch casserole. Bake until fish flakes easily when tested with fork. Serve on bed of rice. Garnish with parsley and lemon slices. Yield: 6 servings.

Fillet of Sole Pane (above)

155

GOLDEN SALMON CASSEROLE

1 sm. green pepper, chopped	2 c. milk
2 med. onions, chopped	2 c. flaked salmon
3 tbsp. butter or margarine	1 tbsp. lemon juice
4 tbsp. flour	1 c. cooked green peas (opt.)
3/4 tsp. salt	

Saute the green pepper and onions in butter in a saucepan over low heat for 5 minutes or until tender. Blend in the flour and salt. Stir in the milk gradually and bring to a boil, stirring constantly. Cook for 1 minute longer, stirring. Stir in the salmon, lemon juice and peas and pour into a greased 8-inch casserole.

Pimento-Cheese Biscuit Topping

1 c. sifted flour	1/3 to 1/2 c. milk
1 1/2 tsp. baking powder	2 pimentos, chopped
1/2 tsp. salt	3/4 c. grated sharp cheese
3 tbsp. shortening	

Sift the flour with baking powder and salt into a bowl. Cut in the shortening until mixture is consistency of meal. Stir in enough milk to make a soft dough. Knead lightly on a floured board and roll out into a rectangle 1/2 inch thick. Sprinkle with pimentos and cheese. Roll as for jelly roll and cut into 1-inch thick slices. Place on the salmon mixture. Bake at 425 degrees for 20 to 25 minutes or until biscuits are brown. 5-6 servings.

Mrs. E. H. Lee, Corbin, Kentucky

RICE AND SALMON CASSEROLE

1 3/4 c. water	4 tbsp. butter
1 3/4 tsp. salt	4 tbsp. flour
1 1/2 c. packaged precooked rice	Dash of pepper
1 7 3/4-oz. can salmon	2 c. milk
1 c. canned peas	1/2 c. grated American cheese

Bring the water and 1 teaspoon salt to a boil in a saucepan and stir in rice. Cover and remove from heat. Let stand for 5 minutes. Drain and flake the salmon. Arrange alternate layers of rice, salmon and peas in a greased 1 1/2-quart casserole. Melt the butter in a saucepan and blend in flour, remaining salt and pepper. Add the milk gradually and cook over medium heat, stirring constantly, until thickened. Pour over the casserole and sprinkle with cheese. Bake at 350 degrees for about 20 minutes or until cheese is melted.

Mrs. Gladys Mason, Roanoke, Virginia

SALMON CASSEROLE

1 1-lb. can salmon	1 med. onion, chopped
1 4-oz. package egg noodles	1/2 c. sliced pitted ripe olives

| 1 c. cheese soup | 1 1-lb. can peas, drained |
| 1 1/2 tsp. Worcestershire sauce | |

Drain the salmon and reserve liquid. Flake the salmon. Cook the noodles according to package directions and drain. Combine the noodles, onion, olives, soup, reserved liquid and Worcestershire sauce in a bowl. Add the salmon and peas and mix lightly. Place in a casserole. Bake at 350 degrees for about 30 minutes or until heated through.

Mrs. J. M. Forbus, Hogansville, Georgia

SCALLOPS WITH GRAPES

Margarine	1/8 tsp. cayenne pepper
1 lb. sea scallops, sliced	1/8 tsp. garlic powder
2 sm. onions, chopped	2 egg yolks
1 tbsp. cornstarch	1/2 c. light cream
1 c. seedless white grapes	1/2 to 1 c. fine dry bread
1 tbsp. chopped parsley	crumbs
1/2 tsp. salt	1 tsp. paprika

Melt 2 tablespoons margarine in a 10-inch skillet over medium heat. Add the scallops and saute, stirring frequently, for 10 minutes. Drain the scallops and add enough water to liquid to make 1 cup. Set aside. Melt 2 tablespoons margarine in a 2-quart saucepan over medium heat, then add the onions and cook until golden. Mix the cornstarch into the onion mixture. Remove from heat. Add the scallop liquid gradually and cook, stirring constantly, until mixture comes to a boil and boils for 1 minute. Reduce the heat to low and add the scallops, grapes, parsley, salt, cayenne pepper and garlic powder. Beat the egg yolks with cream until well blended, then stir into the scallop mixture gradually and cook until thickened. Turn into a shallow 2 1/2-quart baking dish. Toss the bread crumbs with 2 tablespoons melted margarine and the paprika. Sprinkle over the scallops. Bake in 400-degree oven for 5 minutes. 6 servings.

Scallops with Grapes (above)

ASPARAGUS AND SHRIMP

2 med. cans asparagus	1 can pimento strips, drained
1 1/2 c. cooked rice	1 can cream of mushroom soup
1 can sliced mushrooms, drained	Pepper to taste
	1/2 c. milk
1 1/2 lb. cleaned cooked shrimp	1 c. grated cheese

Drain the asparagus and reserve 1/4 cup liquid. Place the rice in a greased shallow baking dish and place the asparagus on rice. Spread mushrooms over the asparagus, then add the shrimp and pimentos. Mix the soup with pepper, milk and reserved liquid and pour over baking dish. Sprinkle with cheese. Bake in 400-degree oven for about 20 minutes or until brown. 6-8 servings.

Mrs. Robert G. Molloy, Alexandria, Louisiana

BROWN RICE AND SHRIMP CASSEROLE

2 lb. cleaned cooked shrimp	3 tbsp. grated onion
2 1/2 c. cooked brown rice	2 tbsp. chopped green pepper
1 c. mayonnaise	Salt and pepper to taste
1 1/2 tsp. Worcestershire sauce	1 lge. can green peas, drained
	Toasted bread crumbs

Combine all ingredients except the crumbs and place in a baking dish. Cover with crumbs. Bake at 350 degrees for 30 to 40 minutes.

Mrs. E. P. Sealy, Jr., Ralph, Alabama

GOLDEN SHRIMP CASSEROLE

5 slices buttered bread	1/2 tsp. dry mustard
3 c. cleaned cooked shrimp	1/2 tsp. salt
2 c. grated American cheese	1/8 tsp. pepper
3 eggs, beaten	Dash of paprika
2 c. milk	

Cut the bread into small cubes. Place alternate layers of bread cubes, shrimp and cheese in a 1 1/2-quart casserole. Mix the eggs with milk in a bowl and stir in remaining ingredients. Pour over the casserole and place in a shallow pan of hot water. Bake at 325 degrees for 1 hour and 20 minutes. 6-8 servings.

Mrs. N. P. Heath, Shreveport, Louisiana

EGGPLANT-SHRIMP CASSEROLE

2 med. eggplant, cooked	1/2 c. chopped green pepper
1 lb. shelled deveined shrimp	1/2 c. chopped parsley
1 c. cubed French bread	1/4 c. chopped celery

1 lge. onion, chopped fine	2 slices bacon, diced
2 garlic cloves, chopped fine	2 tbsp. margarine
Salt and pepper to taste	1 c. bread crumbs

Mash the eggplant in a large mixing bowl. Cut the shrimp in small pieces and add to eggplant. Wet the bread cubes and squeeze dry. Add to eggplant mixture. Add the green pepper, parsley, celery, onion, garlic, salt and pepper and mix well. Cook the bacon in a large kettle until partially done. Add the eggplant mixture and cook over low heat, stirring frequently, for about 20 minutes. Add 1 table-spoon margarine and stir well. Place in large casserole and top with bread crumbs. Dot with remaining margarine. Bake at 350 degrees for about 20 minutes or until browned. 6 servings.

Mrs. Rose Singer, New Orleans, Louisiana

SCALLOPED AVOCADO AND SHRIMP

1 can Cheddar cheese soup	2 c. hot cooked rice
1/2 c. milk	1 avocado
1 4 1/2-oz. can shrimp, drained	1/2 c. grated Parmesan cheese

Mix the soup and milk in a saucepan and bring to boiling point, stirring occasionally. Stir in the shrimp. Spread the rice in a shallow baking dish. Cut the avocado lengthwise into halves and remove seed. Peel and slice. Place over the rice and cover with shrimp mixture. Sprinkle with Parmesan cheese. Bake in 325-degree oven for about 20 minutes.

Mrs. S. A. Lovgren, Freeport, Texas

SHRIMP HARPIN

2 1/2 lb. large shrimp	1/8 tsp. pepper
1 tbsp. lemon juice	Dash of cayenne pepper
3 tbsp. salad oil	1/8 tsp. mace
3/4 c. rice	1 can tomato soup
1/4 c. minced green pepper	1 c. heavy cream
1/4 c. minced onion	1/2 c. sherry
2 tbsp. butter	3/4 c. slivered blanched
1 tsp. salt	almonds

Cook the shrimp in boiling, salted water for 5 minutes, then drain. Place in a 2-quart casserole and sprinkle with lemon juice and salad oil. Cook the rice according to package directions and drain. Chill. Reserve 8 shrimp. Saute the green pepper and onion in butter in a skillet for 5 minutes. Add the rice, salt, pepper, cayenne pepper, mace, soup, cream, sherry and 1/2 cup almonds and mix with the shrimp in casserole. Bake at 350 degrees for 35 minutes. Top with reserved shrimp and remaining almonds and bake for 20 minutes longer or until bubbly and brown. 6-8 servings.

Mrs. Charles W. Strangward, Sylvester, Georgia

SHRIMP BUFFET CASSEROLE

1/2 c. chopped green pepper	1 can tomato soup
1/2 c. chopped onion	3/4 c. light cream
2 tbsp. margarine	1/4 c. sherry
3 c. cleaned cooked shrimp	3/4 tsp. salt
1 tbsp. lemon juice	1/4 tsp. nutmeg
2 c. cooked rice	

Cook the green pepper and onion in the margarine in a saucepan until onion is soft. Stir in remaining ingredients and pour into a 2-quart casserole. Bake at 350 degrees for 30 minutes. Garnish with toasted almonds and parsley. 6 servings.

Mrs. Abbott Y. Wilcox, Jr., St. Petersburg, Florida

GARDEN HARVEST SHRIMP CASSEROLE

4 cloves of garlic	5 lge. tomatoes
2 lge. sweet onions	1/2 c. olive oil
5 med. green peppers	1 tbsp. salt
1 med. eggplant	1/2 tsp. freshly ground pepper
1 1/2 tbsp. lemon juice	2 lb. cleaned shrimp
5 sm. zucchini	

Peel the garlic and mince. Peel the onions and slice thin, then separate into rings. Cut the green peppers into 1-inch wedges and discard the seeds and stems. Peel the eggplant and slice 1/4 inch thick, then sprinkle with the lemon juice. Remove ends from the zucchini and slice thin. Peel the tomatoes and slice thin. Pour 1/4 cup of the olive oil in a Dutch oven, then add half the garlic and simmer for 1 minute. Add half the onions and cook for 1 minute longer, without browning. Combine the salt and pepper and sprinkle a small amount over the

Garden Harvest Shrimp Casserole (above)

onions. Arrange half the green pepper, eggplant, zucchini, shrimp and tomatoes in layers in the Dutch oven, sprinkling each layer with the salt and pepper mixture, then sprinkle with a small amount of the remaining garlic and remaining olive oil. Repeat the layers, beginning with onions and ending with the shrimp and tomatoes. Sprinkle with the remaining garlic and the remaining oil. Bring to a boil, then reduce the heat to a fast simmer and cover. Cook for 20 minutes. Remove the cover and cook for 10 to 20 minutes longer or until the green pepper is tender. Sauce may be thickened with 2 teaspoons flour, if desired.

SHRIMP CREOLE CASSEROLE

2 c. rice	1 No. 2 can tomatoes
2 tbsp. butter	2 cans shrimp, drained
1/2 c. chopped celery	2 tbsp. Worcestershire sauce
1/2 c. chopped onion	4 hard-boiled eggs, chopped
1/2 c. chopped green peppers	Salt and pepper to taste

Cook the rice according to package directions, then drain. Melt the butter in a saucepan. Add celery, onion and green peppers and cook until tender. Add the tomatoes, shrimp, Worcestershire sauce, rice, eggs, salt and pepper and mix lightly. Pour into a casserole. Bake at 350 degrees for 30 minutes or until slightly browned.

Mrs. Elizabeth W. Foy, Gastonia, North Carolina

SHRIMP DE JONGHE

1 c. butter	Dash of cayenne pepper
2 cloves of garlic, minced	1/2 c. cooking sherry
1/3 c. chopped parsley	4 lb. cleaned cooked shrimp
1/2 tsp. paprika	2 c. soft bread crumbs

Melt the butter in a saucepan. Add the garlic, parsley, paprika, cayenne pepper and sherry and mix well. Cover. Simmer for 25 minutes. Add the shrimp and crumbs and stir lightly. Place in a casserole. Bake at 325 degrees for 25 to 30 minutes. Garnish with additional parsley. 8 servings.

Mrs. Dorothy DuBose, Selma, Alabama

SHRIMP NEPTUNE

2 lb. cleaned cooked shrimp	1 7-oz. can green peas,
1/4 c. sliced ripe olives	drained
1 1/2 c. toasted bread cubes	1/2 c. sour cream
3/4 tsp. salt	1 c. mayonnaise

Place the shrimp in a large bowl. Add the olives, bread cubes, salt and peas and mix. Combine the sour cream and mayonnaise. Add to the shrimp mixture and mix. Place in a greased casserole. Bake at 400 degrees for 25 minutes. 6 servings.

Mrs. Robert Fogle, Orangeburg, South Carolina

SHRIMP PILAF

1 c. rice	1 1/4 c. beef bouillon
3 tbsp. butter or margarine	3 tbsp. minced parsley
1 med. onion, diced	1/4 tsp. cayenne pepper
3/4 c. chopped green pepper	1/4 tsp. summer savory
1 c. diced celery	1/2 tsp. salt
3 c. tomato juice	1 lb. cleaned cooked shrimp

Cook the rice in butter in a large skillet until golden, stirring occasionally. Stir in the onion, green pepper, celery, tomato juice and bouillon. Place in a casserole and cover tightly. Bake at 375 degrees for 30 minutes. Add remaining ingredients and stir. Bake for 20 minutes longer.

Mrs. Betsey Walker, San Antonio, Texas

SPICY SHRIMP CASSEROLE

1/3 c. finely chopped onion	1 sm. bay leaf
1 clove of garlic, pressed	3 tbsp. chopped parsley
2 tbsp. butter or margarine	1/2 tsp. cloves
2 lb. shrimp, shelled and deveined	1/2 tsp. marjoram
1 c. rice	1 tsp. chili powder
1 No. 2 1/2 can tomatoes	Dash of cayenne pepper
2 c. chicken broth	1 tsp. salt
	1/8 tsp. pepper

Brown the onion and garlic in butter in a saucepan, then place in a casserole. Add the shrimp, rice, tomatoes, chicken broth, bay leaf, parsley, cloves, marjoram, chili powder, cayenne pepper, salt and pepper and mix well. Cover. Bake at 350 degrees for 1 hour and 30 minutes. 6 servings.

Mrs. Robert J. Kasper, Menlo Park, California

TASTY EGGPLANT AND SHRIMP

1/2 c. butter	6 slices toasted bread
2 lge. onions, chopped	4 eggs
2 cloves of garlic, chopped	1 3-lb. package frozen shrimp
5 eggplant	3 sprigs of parsley
1 tsp. salt	

Melt the butter in a heavy skillet. Add the onions and garlic and cook until onions are soft. Peel the eggplant and cook in boiling, salted water until tender. Drain and mash. Add the salt. Dip the bread into water and squeeze out excess moisture. Add to the eggplant. Add the onion mixture and eggs. Cook the shrimp in boiling, salted water until pink. Drain and cool. Shell and devein the shrimp and stir into the eggplant mixture. Pour into greased baking dishes. Bake at 350 degrees for 1 hour. Garnish with parsley.

Mrs. John W. Jones, Corinth, Mississippi

AVOCADO-TUNA CASSEROLE

2 med. ripe avocados	1/2 c. diced Cheddar cheese
2 6 1/2-oz. cans tuna, drained	Juice of 1 lemon
1/2 c. finely chopped onions	2 tbsp. melted butter
3/4 c. fine bread crumbs	1 can cream of mushroom soup

Peel and slice the avocados. Arrange alternate layers of avocados, tuna, onions, bread crumbs and cheese in a greased medium casserole. Pour lemon juice and butter over top and add the soup. Bake at 375 degrees for 25 minutes. 6 servings.

Mrs. R. R. Raymond, Fallbrook, California

DEVILED TUNA

4 tbsp. butter or margarine	1 tsp. Worcestershire sauce
1/2 sm. onion, chopped	2 tsp. lemon juice
4 stalks celery, chopped	Hot sauce to taste
2 tbsp. flour	2 pimentos, chopped
1/2 tsp. dry mustard	2 hard-cooked eggs, chopped
1/2 tsp. salt	2 7-oz. cans tuna
1 c. milk	1/2 c. soft bread crumbs

Preheat oven to 400 degrees. Melt 2 tablespoons butter in a saucepan. Add the onion and celery and cook until tender. Add flour, mustard and salt. Stir in milk and cook, stirring constantly, until thick. Add the Worcestershire sauce, lemon juice, hot sauce, pimentos and eggs. Drain the tuna and stir into egg mixture. Melt remaining butter and mix with crumbs. Fill baking shells or ramekins with tuna mixture and sprinkle buttered crumbs around edges. Bake for 20 minutes. 6 servings.

Mrs. Thelma E. Ekholm, Fort Worth, Texas

TUNA-MUSHROOM SCALLOP

1 4-oz. can mushrooms	1/4 tsp. pepper
Milk	2 tbsp. grated onion
4 tbsp. shortening	1 8-oz. package potato chips, crushed
4 tbsp. flour	1 can drained tuna, flaked
1 tsp. salt	

Drain the mushrooms and reserve liquid. Add enough milk to the reserved liquid to make 2 cups liquid. Melt the shortening in a saucepan. Add the flour, salt and pepper and blend well. Add the milk mixture slowly and cook, stirring constantly, until thickened. Add the onion and mix well. Place 1/3 of the potato chips in a 10 x 6 x 2-inch greased casserole and cover with the tuna. Add the mushrooms, then the sauce. Add remaining potato chips. Bake in 350-degree oven for 35 to 45 minutes. 6 servings.

Mrs. Gladys Hall, Apopka, Florida

TUNA-BROCCOLI CASSEROLE

1 7-oz. can tuna	Milk
1 package frozen broccoli	Dash of salt
1 can cream of mushroom soup	2 c. biscuit mix

Drain and flake the tuna. Cook the broccoli according to package directions and drain. Cut off 1/4 cup flowerets and reserve. Cut remaining broccoli into bite-sized pieces. Place in a greased 9-inch square pan and cover with tuna. Mix the soup, 1/2 cup milk and salt and pour over the tuna. Mix 2/3 cup milk with biscuit mix in a bowl and stir in reserved broccoli. Drop from teaspoon onto broccoli mixture. Bake at 450 degrees for 15 minutes. 6 servings.

Mrs. E. A. Berger, San Angelo, Texas

TUNA-CORN BREAD CASSEROLE

1 6 1/2-oz. can tuna	1 can cream of mushroom soup
1/2 c. bread crumbs	1 1/4 c. milk
2 tbsp. chopped onion	2 tbsp. melted butter
3 eggs, beaten	1 1/2 c. self-rising cornmeal

Drain and mash the tuna and place in a bowl. Add the crumbs, onion, 2 eggs and soup and mix well. Spoon into a greased casserole. Mix the milk, remaining egg and butter in a bowl. Add the cornmeal and blend until smooth. Spoon over the tuna mixture. Bake in 400-degree oven for about 30 minutes or until brown. 4-5 servings.

Fran Dedmon, Brownsville, Tennessee

TUNA ROMANOFF

1 c. cottage cheese	1 tbsp. Worcestershire sauce
1 c. sour cream	1/4 tsp. hot sauce
2 tbsp. minced onion	2 c. cooked noodles
2 tbsp. chopped pimento	2 cans grated tuna
1 tbsp. lemon juice	1/2 c. sliced ripe olives

Combine the cottage cheese, sour cream, onion, pimento, lemon juice, Worcestershire sauce and hot sauce in a bowl. Stir in the noodles, tuna and olives and place in a greased 2-quart casserole. Bake at 350 degrees for 40 minutes. 6 servings.

Mrs. Hal Ikner, Savannah, Georgia

TUNA-TOMATO CASSEROLE

1 6 1/2-oz. can tuna	6 lge. ripe pitted olives,
1 6-oz. package medium	sliced
noodles	1 can cream of tomato soup
2 tbsp. minced onion	1/4 c. milk
1/4 tsp. salt	1/4 c. grated sharp cheese

Drain and flake the tuna. Cook the noodles in boiling, salted water until tender, then drain. Combine tuna with the onion, salt, olives, soup and milk. Place half the noodles in a greased 1 1/2-quart casserole and cover with tuna mixture. Add remaining noodles and sprinkle with cheese. Bake at 350 degrees for 30 minutes.

Claudia Cato, Oak Grove, Louisiana

TUNA BAKE

1 6-oz. package noodles	1 can chicken soup
1 can tuna	1 1/2-lb. package sliced sharp
3 hard-boiled eggs, sliced	cheese

Cook the noodles according to package directions and drain. Place in a 9-inch square casserole. Add the tuna, then the eggs. Pour the soup over the eggs. Cut the cheese into cubes and place over the soup. Bake at 325 degrees for 25 minutes.

Mrs. G. P. Grogan, Atlanta, Georgia

TONNO EGGPLANT PARMIGIANA

2 7-oz. cans tuna in oil	1/2 tsp. oregano
Olive oil	1 8-oz. can tomato sauce
1 lge. eggplant, sliced	1/2 c. grated Parmesan cheese
1/2 tsp. basil	8 oz. sliced mozzarella cheese

Drain the oil from the tuna into a measuring cup and add olive oil to make 1/2 cup, then pour into a skillet. Brown the eggplant in the oil and drain well on paper towels. Layer half the eggplant and 1 can of tuna in a 1 1/2-quart casserole. Stir the basil and oregano into tomato sauce and cover the tuna with half the sauce. Sprinkle with half the Parmesan cheese and cover with half the mozzarella cheese slices. Repeat layers, ending with mozzarella cheese. Bake at 350 degrees for 30 minutes. 6 servings.

Tonno Eggplant Parmigiana (above)

seafood sauces and stuffings

Adding an extra measure of flair and elegance to your fish and shellfish dishes are sauces and stuffings. They boost the mild seafood flavors with many outstanding ingredients. And whether highly seasoned or mild in taste, hot or cold, both sauces and stuffings should always complement the fine flavor of the seafood.

In general, light and mild sauces go well with fresh- and salt-water fish, zesty sauces with shellfish. But this is not a hard and fast rule since the cooking method you use is also an important consideration. For broiled fish, you may want to try Sauce Meuniere or Tartar Sauce Supreme. Both of these sauces have a high fat content that replaces some of the natural moisture lost from the fish during cooking. For baked or poached fish, a well seasoned sauce such as Caper Sauce or Fish Sauce is recommended.

Seafood stuffings are also a matter of individual taste, though here, too, compatibility is an important factor. Used mostly in baked seafood dishes, stuffings are of two major types, which usually contain finely chopped vegetables, seasonings, and a binding ingredient. Rice and wild rice are two popular seafood stuffing bases as are dried bread crumbs.

Sauces and stuffings are the special touches that add so much to your seafood dishes. Turn to this chapter again and again for delicious and elegant recipes.

167

BEARNAISE SAUCE

4 egg yolks	1/4 c. light cream
2 tbsp. tarragon vinegar	1/2 c. butter
Salt and cayenne pepper to taste	1/4 c. chopped parsley
	Minced garlic to taste

Combine the egg yolks, vinegar, salt, cayenne pepper and cream in top of a double boiler. Place over hot water and cook, stirring constantly, until thickened. Stir in the butter, parsley and garlic and cook until the butter is melted. Serve with oysters.

Elva Gloria Ruiz, Buckholts, Texas

BURNED CURRY SAUCE

4 tbsp. curry	4 tbsp. minced parsley
1 tbsp. horseradish	5 tbsp. lemon juice
3 tbsp. minced onion	1 qt. mayonnaise

Cook the curry in a saucepan over high heat, stirring constantly, until almost black. Have exhaust fan on and keep the saucepan on burner at back of stove to avoid breathing fumes. Cool. Combine 2 tablespoons burned curry with remaining ingredients in a bowl and mix well. Chill. Serve with shrimp.

Mrs. Sally Galloway, Laurel, Mississippi

CAPER SAUCE

2 tbsp. butter	1 1/2 c. milk
1/4 c. chopped onion	2 tbsp. lemon juice
2 tbsp. flour	2 tbsp. drained capers
1/2 tsp. salt	1 tbsp. chopped parsley

Melt the butter in a saucepan. Add the onion and saute until tender. Blend in flour and salt. Add the milk slowly and cook, stirring constantly, until smooth and thickened. Stir in the lemon juice, capers and parsley. Serve with baked, stuffed fish.

Mrs. William Hall, Panama City, Florida

ANCHOVY SAUCE FOR SEAFOOD

2 tbsp. anchovy paste	1/4 c. chili sauce or catsup
1 tbsp. tarragon vinegar	1/2 c. chopped celery
1 c. mayonnaise	1 tbsp. lemon juice

Mix the anchovy paste and vinegar in a bowl until smooth. Add remaining ingredients and mix well.

Frances Watts, Flagstaff, Arizona

Scallop Sauce (below)

SCALLOP SAUCE

1/4 c. finely chopped celery	2 tbsp. prepared mustard
1/4 c. corn oil	2 tbsp. cider vinegar
1 clove of garlic	1/2 tsp. salt
3 tbsp. minced onion	1/2 tsp. sugar

Place all the ingredients in a jar, then cover and shake. Refrigerate for several hours, then remove the garlic. Mix well and use as basting sauce for scallops and any remaining sauce may be served with grilled scallops. About 3/4 cup.

COCKTAIL SAUCE FOR ROCK LOBSTER

1 bottle chili sauce	1 tsp. Worcestershire sauce
1/2 bottle catsup	6 tbsp. horseradish
2 tbsp. maple syrup	2 tbsp. lemon juice

Combine all ingredients and mix well. Serve with sliced cooked South African rock lobster-tails.

Photograph for this recipe on page 166.

BOILED SHRIMP SAUCE

	1 tsp. Worcestershire sauce
1 c. catsup	Dash of hot sauce
1/2 c. lemon juice	1 tsp. horseradish
1 tsp. salt	

Mix all ingredients in a bowl and chill. Serve with shrimp.

Mrs. Bill Stubbs, Greenwood, Mississippi

LIME COCKTAIL SAUCE FOR SHELLFISH

2 tbsp. prepared horseradish	6 tbsp. lime juice
1 c. catsup	1/4 tsp. hot sauce
1 tsp. salt	

Mix all ingredients in a bowl and chill. Serve with oysters or clams.

Mrs. M. D. Sinback, North Ft. Myers, Florida

OYSTER COCKTAIL SAUCE

1 c. catsup	2 tsp. lemon juice
1 sm. onion, grated	1 tbsp. Worcestershire sauce
2 tbsp. finely chopped celery	

Combine all ingredients in a bowl and chill for at least 30 minutes. Serve with oysters.

Mrs. Raymond Brooks, Hamburg, Arkansas

COCKTAIL SAUCE ANGOSTURA

3/4 c. catsup	2 tsp. mustard seed
1/4 c. minced celery	1 tsp. angostura aromatic
1 tsp. sugar	bitters

Cocktail Sauce Angostura (above)

Blend all ingredients together thoroughly and chill. Pour over diced South African rock lobster meat.

REMOULADE SAUCE

1 c. mayonnaise	1 tbsp. horseradish
1 tbsp. chopped onion	1 tsp. paprika
1 tbsp. chopped parsley	1/2 tsp. salt
1 tbsp. chopped celery	Dash of hot sauce
2 tbsp. mustard	1/4 c. salad oil
1 tbsp. vinegar	1/2 tsp. Worcestershire sauce

Combine all ingredients in a small bowl and blend well. Refrigerate for several hours or overnight. Serve with boiled shrimp, crab meat or lobster. 1 1/2 cups.

Mrs. Jerry Roberson, Columbia, Tennessee

SEAFOOD DIPPING SAUCE

1/2 c. mayonnaise	1 tsp. mustard
1/4 c. cocktail sauce	1 tbsp. grated onion

Mix all ingredients in a bowl and chill.

Greta Tucker, Albuquerque, New Mexico

SHRIMP SAUCE

1/2 c. catsup	5 drops of hot sauce
1/2 c. mayonnaise	1 clove of garlic, pressed
2 tsp. grated onion	

Combine all ingredients in a bowl and chill. Serve with shrimp. 1 cup.

Mrs. Judy Smith, Montgomery, Alabama

CREOLE SAUCE FOR SHRIMP

1 c. chopped onions	1 6-oz. can tomato paste
1 c. chopped green pepper	1 can cream of tomato soup
1 c. diagonally sliced celery	1 tsp. salt
1 clove of garlic, minced	1 tsp. sugar
4 tbsp. butter	1/2 tsp. thyme

Cook the onions, green pepper, celery and garlic in butter in a saucepan until tender. Blend in remaining ingredients and simmer for 10 minutes or until thick. Serve with shrimp. 6 servings.

Mrs. Curtis Thomas, Fort Worth, Texas

FISH SAUCE

1/2 c. grated American or Parmesan cheese	1/2 c. grated Swiss cheese
	1 recipe white sauce

Combine the cheeses and white sauce in top of double boiler. Place over hot water and cook, stirring, until cheese is melted. Serve with fish.

Mrs. V. A. Cleveland, Paducah, Kentucky

HORSERADISH SAUCE

3 tbsp. horseradish	1/2 tsp. salt
1/2 c. heavy cream, whipped	

Fold the horseradish into whipped cream and season with salt.

Lucy Parks, Oklahoma City, Oklahoma

LEMON-BUTTER SAUCE

1/2 c. butter	Salt to taste
1/4 c. lemon juice	

Melt the butter in a saucepan. Stir in the lemon juice and heat through. Add the salt and keep warm.

Mrs. Henry Gates, Dothan, Alabama

ZESTY LEMON SAUCE

3 tbsp. butter	1 tbsp. steak sauce
5 tbsp. sifted flour	1/2 tsp. grated onion
1 c. milk	1/4 tsp. salt
1/4 tsp. celery salt	1/8 tsp. pepper
1 tbsp. lemon juice	

Melt the butter in a saucepan and stir in the flour. Stir in the milk slowly and add remaining ingredients. Cook over low heat until thick, stirring constantly.

Mrs. Willis McNeely, Dublin, Georgia

MUSHROOM SAUCE

1 pt. fresh mushrooms, sliced	1 c. water
1/4 c. melted butter	1 chicken bouillon cube
2 tbsp. flour	1 tbsp. chopped pimento
Salt and pepper to taste	

Brown the mushrooms lightly in the butter in a saucepan and blend in the flour, salt and pepper. Add the water and bouillon cube and bring to a boil, stirring constantly. Stir in the pimento and cook for 1 minute longer. One 6-ounce can broiled-in-butter mushrooms may be substituted for fresh mushrooms.

Mrs. Donald H. Eller, Claremont, Virginia

SAUCE FOR SHRIMP

2 tbsp. butter	1 tbsp. Worcestershire sauce
2 tbsp. flour	3 dashes of hot sauce
1 c. cream	Salt and pepper to taste
3 tbsp. catsup	

Melt the butter in a saucepan and stir in the flour. Stir in the cream and cook, stirring, until thickened. Add remaining ingredients and heat through.

Mrs. Sam Steele, Raleigh, North Carolina

SAUCE FOR FRIED SHRIMP

1 c. catsup	1/2 tsp. salt
1/4 c. Worcestershire sauce	Dash of pepper
1 tsp. hot sauce	

Combine all ingredients in a bowl and mix well. Serve with fried shrimp. 4 servings.

Mrs. John Futch, Aiken, South Carolina

SAUCE MEUNIERE

1/2 c. butter	1/2 tsp. salt
1 tbsp. minced parsley	1/4 tsp. pepper
1 tbsp. minced green onion	Dash of hot sauce
2 tbsp. lemon juice	Dash of Worcestershire sauce

Place all ingredients in a small saucepan and cook over low heat until butter is melted, stirring constantly. Serve with fish.

Mrs. John Myers, Natchitoches, Louisiana

LOBSTER SAUCE FOR SPAGHETTI

2 cans lobster	1 sprig of parsley
1/3 c. cooking oil	Salt and pepper to taste
1 clove of garlic, pressed	1 can tomato sauce

Drain the lobster and cut into pieces. Heat the oil in a saucepan. Add the garlic and cook until brown. Add the lobster, parsley, salt and pepper and tomato sauce and simmer until thickened. Serve over spaghetti.

Mrs. R. N. Walther, Baltimore, Maryland

Spaghetti with White Clam Sauce (below)

SPAGHETTI WITH WHITE CLAM SAUCE

4 doz. cherrystone clams	1/3 c. chopped parsley
4 tbsp. salt	4 cloves of garlic, minced
1 c. cornmeal	Freshly ground pepper to taste
1/4 c. butter	1 lb. spaghetti
1/4 c. olive oil	

Scrub the clams with a brush under cold running water, then place clams in large pot and add 2 tablespoons salt, cornmeal and 5 quarts cold water. Chill for 2 hours. Drain and rinse the clams, then drain again. Place the clams in a shallow pan. Bake at 350 degrees for 5 to 10 minutes or just until shells open slightly. Open clams with a sharp knife and scrape out the meat into a colander placed over a bowl. Pour all the clam juice in shells and pan into colander. Pick over clams or wash to remove any bits of shell. Allow the clams to drain well, then chop coarsely and set aside. Pour the clam juice into a saucepan and simmer until reduced to 1 1/2 cups. Combine the butter, oil, parsley and garlic in a large saucepan over medium heat and cook for 2 minutes, stirring occasionally. Add the clam broth and clams and simmer, uncovered, for about 3 minutes. Season with pepper. Add the remaining salt to 5 quarts rapidly boiling water in a large kettle, then add the spaghetti gradually so water continues to boil. Cook, uncovered, stirring occasionally, until tender. Drain in colander. Serve in shallow bowls topped with clam sauce.

SEAFOOD SAUCE FOR TROUT

2 egg yolks	1 c. cleaned cooked shrimp,
1 c. melted butter	chopped
1 tbsp. lemon juice	1/2 c. flaked cooked crab meat

1/2 c. sliced mushrooms
1 tbsp. flour
1/4 c. dry white wine

Paprika to taste
Salt and pepper to taste

Place the egg yolks in top of a double boiler and beat well. Place over hot water. Add the butter gradually and cook, stirring constantly, until thickened. Add the lemon juice, shrimp, crab meat, mushrooms and flour and mix well. Stir in the wine and seasonings and cook for 15 minutes, stirring frequently. Serve with trout.

Lorraine Milling, Columbia, South Carolina

TUNA ITALIENNE SAUCE

1 7-oz. can solid-pack tuna
   in oil
1/2 c. chopped onion

1 clove of garlic, chopped fine
1 c. tomato sauce
2 tbsp. minced parsley

Drain the tuna and reserve the oil. Place the reserved oil in a saucepan and heat. Add the onion and garlic and cook over low heat until lightly browned. Add the tuna and tomato sauce. Cook over low heat for about 15 minutes or until thickened, stirring occasionally. Add the parsley. Serve over spaghetti.

Mrs. Claude W. Rahm, New Orleans, Louisiana

ZIPPY SHRIMP WITH SPAGHETTI

2 cloves of garlic, minced
1/4 c. cooking oil
1 14-oz. can tomatoes
2 1/2 tsp. salt
1/2 tsp. dried basil
1 6-oz. can tomato paste
1 tsp. dried oregano

1/2 lb. cooked shelled shrimp,
   deveined
1/2 tsp. garlic salt
1 tsp. prepared horseradish
1 8-oz. package spaghetti
Grated Parmesan cheese

Brown the garlic in oil in a saucepan. Add the tomatoes, salt and basil and simmer for 30 minutes. Stir in tomato paste and oregano and simmer for 15 minutes. Stir in the shrimp, garlic salt and horseradish and heat through. Cook the spaghetti according to package directions and drain. Serve shrimp mixture over hot spaghetti and sprinkle with cheese. 4 servings.

Elizabeth Miller, Fulton, Mississippi

TARTAR SAUCE SUPREME

1 c. mayonnaise
1 1/2 tbsp. minced pickles
1 1/2 tbsp. minced parsley

1 1/2 tbsp. capers
1 1/2 tbsp. grated onion
1 1/2 tbsp. minced green olives

Combine all ingredients in a bowl and chill for several hours. 1 cup.

Mrs. Janice C. Brown, Tyler, Texas

Low-Calorie Creole Sauce (below)

LOW-CALORIE CREOLE SAUCE

2 c. canned stewed tomatoes	2 bouillon cubes
2 tbsp. chopped onion	2 grated carrots
2 tbsp. minced celery leaves	1 tsp. angostura aromatic
2 tbsp. chopped green pepper	bitters
2 tbsp. minced parsley	Salt and pepper to taste

Combine the tomatoes, onion, celery leaves, green pepper, parsley and 1 cup water in a saucepan. Add the crushed bouillon cubes and bring to a boil. Simmer for 30 minutes. Add the carrots, bitters, salt and pepper. Serve with lobster-tails or shrimp. About 3 cups.

EASY TARTAR SAUCE

1 c. mayonnaise	1 tsp. chopped parsley
1 tbsp. grated onion	1 tsp. chopped pimento
1 tbsp. minced dill pickle	

Combine all ingredients in a bowl and cover. Chill for several hours. Serve with seafood.

Mrs. Marolyn K. Whitehead, Miami, Florida

TARTAR SAUCE FOR FISH

1 pt. mayonnaise	1 1/2 tbsp. finely chopped
1/4 c. mustard	garlic
1/4 c. parsley flakes	Juice of 1/2 lemon
1/4 c. capers	3/4 c. salad oil
1/4 tube anchovy paste	

Mix first 7 ingredients in a bowl. Beat in oil slowly and chill. 1 quart.

Mrs. Guy Smithson, Marble Falls, Texas

BACON-MUSHROOM STUFFING FOR FISH

6 strips bacon, diced	1 tsp. sage
1/2 c. sliced mushrooms	1 c. chopped shrimp (opt.)
2 c. bread cubes	1/2 tsp. salt
1 tbsp. grated onion	1/8 tsp. pepper
2 tbsp. lemon juice	1 egg
1 tbsp. parsley	

Cook the bacon in a skillet until crisp, then remove from skillet. Saute the mushrooms in the bacon drippings until light brown. Add the bread cubes and cook over low heat until brown. Add the bacon and remaining ingredients and mix well. Stuff fish.

Mrs. Cheryl Lewis, Eufaula, Alabama

ONION STUFFING

3 onions, chopped	1/8 tsp. pepper
1/4 c. cooking oil	2 tbsp. chopped parsley
1 1/2 c. soft bread crumbs	1 egg, beaten
1 tsp. sage	2 tbsp. water
1/2 tsp. salt	

Saute the onions in oil in a saucepan until tender. Add the bread crumbs, sage, salt, pepper and parsley and cook until light brown, stirring frequently. Remove from heat and cool slightly. Stir in the egg and water.

Mrs. Pete Daniels, Little Rock, Arkansas

MUSHROOM-RICE STUFFING

1 16-oz. can sliced mushrooms	1 tsp. garlic powder
2 c. chopped green onions	2 tsp. sweet basil
4 tbsp. butter or margarine	1 tsp. nutmeg
6 c. cooked rice	1 tsp. salt
4 tbsp. chopped parsley	1/2 tsp. pepper

Drain the mushrooms. Saute the onions and mushrooms in butter in a saucepan for about 5 minutes. Add remaining ingredients and toss lightly.

Mrs. S. H. Hastings, Jackson, Mississippi

MUSHROOM DRESSING

1 c. hot water	Onion juice to taste (opt.)
1 1/4 c. bread crumbs	2 tsp. sage
3 tbsp. melted butter	2 eggs
1 tsp. salt	3/4 c. chopped mushrooms

Pour the water over bread crumbs in a bowl, then stir in the butter, salt, onion juice and sage. Beat the eggs and stir into the bread mixture. Add the mushrooms and mix.

Mildred Wise Howe, Dillwyn, Virginia

CRAB-BACON STUFFING

1 c. crab meat	2 slices bacon, diced
2 eggs, slightly beaten	1 c. dry bread crumbs
1 med. onion, chopped	1/4 c. butter
3/4 c. chopped celery	Salt and pepper to taste

Place the crab meat in a bowl and flake. Stir in the eggs. Cook the onion, celery, bacon and bread crumbs in butter in a saucepan over low heat until onion is tender, stirring frequently. Mix with crab mixture and stir in the salt and pepper.

Mrs. J. William Cornelius, Orange Park, Florida

CRAB DRESSING

1 5-oz. can water chestnuts	1/2 c. mayonnaise
1 can mushroom soup	2 7-oz. cans crab
1 1/2 c. packaged stuffing mix	

Drain and slice the water chestnuts. Place in a bowl and stir in the soup, stuffing mix and mayonnaise. Drain and flake the crab, then stir into the soup mixture.

Mrs. Richard A. Hurd, Atlanta, Georgia

CRAB MEAT STUFFING

3 slices bread, cubed	1 tsp. prepared mustard
5 tbsp. milk	1/2 tsp. thyme
2 6 1/2-oz. cans crab meat	1/4 tsp. sage
1/4 tsp. pepper	1/4 c. melted butter
1 tsp. salt	

Soak bread cubes in milk in a bowl. Remove cartilage from the crab meat and mix with bread crumb mixture. Stir in the pepper, salt, mustard, thyme, sage and butter.

Mrs. Bill Anderson, Wheeling, West Virginia

CELERY STUFFING

6 c. toasted bread crumbs	3/4 c. cooking oil
2 1/2 c. diced celery	Salt and pepper to taste
1 sm. onion, minced	3 eggs, slightly beaten
1/2 c. chopped celery leaves	

Place the bread crumbs in a bowl. Cook the celery, onion and celery leaves in oil in a saucepan until tender. Add to crumbs. Add the seasonings and eggs and toss lightly.

Mrs. Bob Bradley, Bowling Green, Kentucky

CRANBERRY STUFFING FOR LOBSTER

8 4-oz. frozen South African rock lobster-tails	2 tbsp. chopped celery
	2 c. small bread cubes
Salt	1 c. fresh cranberries, halved
Pepper to taste	1 tsp. grated lemon rind
Lemon juice to taste	2 tbsp. chopped parsley
4 strips bacon, diced	1 c. tomato juice
2 tbsp. chopped onion	1/2 c. grated Parmesan cheese

Split the frozen lobster-tails lengthwise with a sharp knife cutting through the outer shell, leaving the under membrane intact. Spread open and place in a shallow baking pan. Sprinkle cut surfaces with salt, pepper and lemon juice. Fry the bacon until crisp, then remove the bacon and add the onion and celery to the drippings. Saute until tender. Add the bread cubes and saute until cubes are golden brown. Add the cranberries, lemon rind, parsley and 1 teaspoon salt. Fill the split lobster-tails with cranberry mixture, then spoon tomato juice over stuffing. Sprinkle with Parmesan cheese. Bake at 350 degrees for 20 to 25 minutes or until tops are lightly browned and lobster is done.

Cranberry Stuffing for Lobster (above)

OYSTER DRESSING

1/3 c. butter	1 tsp. salt
1/4 c. minced onion	1/4 tsp. pepper
2 c. crumbled corn bread	1 tsp. sage
2 c. toasted bread crumbs	1 can oysters
1/2 c. chopped celery	1 c. milk

Melt the butter in a large, heavy skillet. Add the onion and cook until tender, stirring occasionally. Turn into a deep bowl. Add remaining ingredients and mix well. One cup fresh oysters may be substituted for canned.

Marie Mottingly, Dawson Springs, Kentucky

OYSTER-RICE DRESSING

1/2 c. chopped onion	3 tbsp. chopped parsley
1/2 c. butter	1 sm. clove of garlic, minced
1 1/2 qt. oysters, drained	1 tsp. salt
3 c. cooked rice	1/2 tsp. paprika
1/2 c. chopped celery	

Saute the onion in butter in a saucepan until tender. Add the oysters and cook until edges curl. Add remaining ingredients and mix well.

Naomi Kinston, Baton Rouge, Louisiana

RICE AND MUSHROOM STUFFING

1/4 c. chopped onions	4 c. cooked wild rice
1 c. sliced mushrooms	1 tsp. salt
1/3 c. butter or margarine	1/2 tsp. pepper

Brown the onions and mushrooms in butter in a saucepan. Add the rice, salt and pepper and mix well.

Mrs. Wilma R. Richardson, Mouth of Wilson, Virginia

SEAFOOD DRESSING FOR FISH

1 can crab meat, drained	1 tsp. onion juice
1 egg, beaten	1 can sm. shrimp, drained
Salt and pepper to taste	Bread crumbs
1/4 c. diced celery	

Mix the crab meat, egg, salt, pepper, celery and onion juice in a bowl and fold in the shrimp. Stir in enough crumbs to hold mixture together.

Mrs. M. J. Newberry, Augusta, Georgia

SESAME STUFFING

2 c. chopped celery and leaves	1/2 tsp. pepper
1 c. chopped onions	3/4 lb. butter or margarine
1 tbsp. parsley flakes	4 qt. toasted bread cubes
4 tbsp. poultry seasoning	3 tbsp. toasted sesame seed
1 tsp. salt	2 c. broth

Saute the celery, onions, parsley and seasonings in butter in a saucepan until the onions are tender. Add the bread and sesame seed and mix. Stir in the broth.

Mrs. Victor Hollingsworth, Tuscaloosa, Alabama

SHRIMP AND RICE DRESSING

1 tbsp. salad oil	2 tbsp. chopped onion tops
1 tbsp. flour	1 1/2 c. boiling water
1 tbsp. minced onion	3 c. cooked rice
1 tbsp. minced celery	3/4 c. shrimp
2 tbsp. chopped parsley	3/4 c. oysters

Heat the oil in a saucepan. Add the flour and cook, stirring, until well browned. Stir in the onion, celery, parsley, onion tops and water and simmer for about 10 minutes. Add the rice, shrimp and oysters and simmer for 15 minutes longer.

Nancy Wade, Miami, Florida

VEGETABLE STUFFING FOR BAKED FISH

1 lge. carrot	1 stalk celery
2 lge. potatoes	1 egg
1 onion	Salt and pepper to taste

Grind the carrot, potatoes, onion and celery through a food chopper, using fine blade, then place in a bowl. Add the egg and seasonings and mix well. Stuff fish.

Mrs. Louise McKinley, Tucson, Arizona

WILD RICE DRESSING

1/2 c. wild rice	Salt and pepper to taste
1 onion, chopped	Sage to taste
2 stalks celery, chopped	2 tbsp. chopped green pepper
1/4 c. butter	2 tbsp. chopped pimento

Prepare the rice according to package directions. Saute the onion and celery in butter in a saucepan until transparent. Add the rice, seasonings, green pepper and pimento and mix well.

Mrs. Ben Browning, Espanola, New Mexico

CHESTNUT DRESSING

2 lb. chestnuts	1 loaf of bread, diced
1 med. onion, diced	1 tbsp. sage
3 lge. stalks celery, diced	Salt and pepper to taste
1 c. chicken broth	

Place the chestnuts in a saucepan and cover with water. Bring to a boil and boil for 10 minutes. Drain, then remove shells and chop. Combine the onion, celery and broth in saucepan and cook until tender. Combine all ingredients, adding water if needed. Stuff a large fish and bake.

Mrs. Ellen Grant, Birmingham, Alabama

EGGPLANT DRESSING

2 eggplant, pared and diced	1 tsp. poultry seasoning
1/2 c. chopped celery	2 eggs
1/2 c. chopped onion	1 tsp. salt
Butter or bacon drippings	1/2 tsp. pepper
1 c. croutons	

Cook the eggplant in salted water until tender, then drain and mash. Saute the celery and onion in butter until tender. Combine all ingredients and mix thoroughly. Stuff fish.

Mrs. Caroline Peak, LaGrange, Georgia

STUFFING FOR TROUT

1 1/2 c. minced onion	1/2 tsp. salt
2 c. diced celery	1/2 tsp. pepper
1/2 c. melted butter	1/2 tsp. sage
2 2/3 c. cooked rice	1/2 tsp. thyme
2 c. chopped stuffed olives	

Saute the onion and celery in butter until tender, then add the remaining ingredients and mix well. Use to stuff a 6 to 8 pound fish.

Mrs. Francis E. Naughton, Fort McPherson, Georgia

STUFFING FOR LOBSTER

1 1/2 c. cracker crumbs	1/2 tsp. salt
1/4 c. melted butter	3 tbsp. chopped parsley
2 tbsp. hot water	

Moisten the crumbs with melted butter and hot water, then add the salt and parsley. Spread dressing generously in cavity and tail of lobster and place on cookie sheet. Bake at 450 degrees for 20 minutes or until lobster is loose in shell.

Mrs. Jane Waters, Arlington, Virginia

Many fish and shellfish fans prefer flavoring their seafood dishes with only salt, pepper, and occasionally lemon. Yet the delicate taste of seafood blends exceptionally well with a variety of herbs, spices, and seeds. Imagination is the key to the successful use of seasonings in seafood cookery. One precaution to observe is to use seasonings sparingly so as not to overwhelm the flavor of the seafood.

The following chart has been prepared for your convenience. It may suggest to you some interesting and imaginative ideas for seasoning seafood. Column one lists in alphabetical order a variety of herbs, spices, and seeds that especially complement the flavor of fish and shellfish. Column two provides a brief description of the appearance and taste of the seasonings. And column three offers suggestions for using the seasonings in cooking.

seasonings

FOR SEAFOOD

SEASONING	DESCRIPTION	USES
Allspice	Small, dried berry whose flavor resembles that of cloves, cinnamon, and nutmeg.	Add to poaching or steaming liquid for both fish and shellfish.
Barbecue seasoning	Blend of many zesty spices such as chili, cumin, garlic, cloves, etc.	Sprinkle over broiling or grilling fish and shellfish.
Basil	Bright green herb with a gently pungent flavor.	Combine with lemon juice for a simple sauce to pour over cooked fish.
Bay leaf	Fragrant dried laurel leaves.	Add to poaching or steaming liquid.
Celery (seed, salt, and flakes)	The flavorful fruit of wild celery.	Add to poaching or steaming liquid; sprinkle on baking fish.
Cloves (ground)	Dried, dark brown, nail-shaped flowerbuds with an exotic flavor.	Sprinkle on fish before baking.
Crab boil or shrimp spice	Includes whole peppercorns, bay leaves, red peppers, mustard seeds, ginger, allspice, savory.	Use with crabs, lobster and shrimp when boiling, baking, or grilling.
Dill seed	Small, sharply flavored, oval-shaped seed.	Add to poaching or steaming liquid.
Ginger (ground)	Light buff root-spice with an unmistakable pungency.	Sprinkle sparingly on cooking fish.

SEASONING	DESCRIPTION	USES
Mace	Exotic red spice with a gentle flavor.	Add to fish sauces or stews and scalloped dishes.
Marjoram	Grayish green herb with a slightly bitter flavor.	Sprinkle on broiling or baking fish; use in sauces.
Mustard (dry)	Yellow or black aromatic seed with a distinctively tangy flavor.	Add to fish sauces, croquettes, and scalloped dishes.
Nutmeg	Warm and sweet spice that is tan in color.	Add to fish cakes and casseroles.
Oregano	Agreeably flavorful and aromatic herb.	Combine with melted butter for use with shellfish.
Paprika	Mild, brilliantly red spice related to pepper.	Add to oil or butter for basting fish; use as a garnish.
Parsley (fresh and dried)	Brilliant green, strong-flavored herb.	Sprinkle generously on cooking fish for a dash of color.
Pickling spice	Blend of mustard, cassia, allspice, dill seed, cloves, turmeric, cardamom, mace.	Sprinkle on broiled fish; add to poaching or steaming liquid.
Rosemary	Grayish-green herb with a pleasant pine flavor.	Flavors fish stocks; sprinkle on broiling or baking fish.
Savory	Small, brownish-green herb with a pungent taste.	Sprinkle on broiling or baking fish; add to fish sauces.
Thyme	Fresh, aromatic herb that is similar in taste to savory.	Combine with stuffings; use in chowders; add to fish before cooking.

Parsley   Cloves   Pepper   Oregano

In addition to the herbs and spices that season seafood during cooking, you should consider the many garnishes that are used in serving seafood. They are attractive and (usually) edible decorations that are added to a serving platter as the finishing touch, thereby providing a colorful contrast to a simple fish fillet or steak.

Choose garnishes that brighten up the platter on which you serve the seafood. Ideally they should provide a definite contrast to the flaky texture and mild flavor of the fish or shellfish. Some of the simplest yet most becoming garnishes include: fresh snipped parsley, watercress, chicory, and endive; lemon or lime wedges; and paprika. Celery and carrot strips gaily surrounded by green pepper or pimento rings add an appetizing crunchiness and a vivid color contrast to broiled or poached fish fillets or steaks. And the briny taste of pickles, stuffed olives, or pickled beet cups provide a distinctively delicious contrast to the mild taste of fish or shellfish.

Buying seafood can be a complicated process because of the huge variety of market forms available. Yet with the general suggestions given below, you can easily learn to recognize quality and freshness. Always purchase your fish and shellfish from a reliable dealer who stakes his reputation on the quality and freshness of his merchandise. Because seafood is a highly perishable commodity, it should be bought as near to the time of preparation as possible. Acquaint yourself with the seasonal variation of many well known varieties of seafood. Purchased at the peak of freshness, they are both economical and exceptionally delicious. However, frozen and iced fish and shellfish are also excellent buys and remarkably fresh-tasting.

HOW TO BUY
seafood

BUYING FISH

In buying fish, learn to judge the quality of your purchase. For fresh *whole fish*, look for bright, clear, bulging eyes; reddish or pink gills; tight shiny scales; firm elastic flesh that springs back when pressed; and a pleasant shore-like odor. *Frozen fish*, that have been cleaned, boned, packed, and quick-frozen at the point of supply, make many varieties conveniently available year-round. The flavor and texture of the fish are exceptionally well preserved during freezing. Check that the package is solidly frozen and contains no evidence of oiliness, discoloration, or freezer burn. Other fish are cleaned and boned soon after they are caught, but packed on ice for shipment throughout the country. This is one of the principal marketing processes for fish fillets and steaks. *Iced fish* are not and should not be frozen; like whole fish, they should smell agreeably fresh and have firm elastic flesh, with no traces of browning or drying around the edges. Whether you are buying bone-in or filleted fish, plan on 1/3 to 1/2 pound edible fish per serving.

BUYING SHELLFISH

Live lobsters should be heavy for their size and a mottled bluish green in color. Have your seafood dealer wedge or fasten the dangerous lobster claws closed. If you purchase cooked lobster, the shell should be brilliantly red and the tail rigidly curled under the body. Fresh shrimp should be slightly green in color and firm to the touch. Usually only the tail portion is marketed.

Fresh clams, oysters, and mussels are also bought live. Their shells should be snapped tightly shut or should close at a touch. Only those with unbroken shells should be selected. Shucked clams and oysters should be plump with no evidence of shrinkage. The liquor in which they are packed should be clear, fresh, and sweet smelling. Scallops are usually sold shucked. They should be virtually free of liquid and have a detectably sweet odor. Look for scallops that are cream-colored rather than white.

Most of the shellfish listed above are also available canned, frozen, iced, and frequently precooked at the market.

MARKET FORMS OF FISH

Being able to judge the quality and freshness of the fish you purchase is the initial step in the buying process. Of equal importance is a familiarity with the various market forms of fresh, iced, and frozen fish. These market forms are: whole, drawn, dressed, steaks, and fillets. They differ principally in the extent of preparation done at the market and the price per pound. Whereas some cuts require further preparation at home (skinning, scaling, eviscerating, etc.), others are ready to cook as they come from the market. By understanding these various forms, you can select cuts appropriate to your cooking plans and your budget. A brief description of each market form with an accompanying illustration is given below.

Whole fish are those marketed just as they come from the water. The scales should be removed before cooking. Small whole fish may be cooked as purchased or they may be eviscerated. Larger whole fish are generally eviscerated; sometimes the head, tail, and fins are also removed and the fish split into serving-size pieces.

Drawn fish are marketed with only the entrails removed. These fish also require scaling before cooking. Small drawn fish may be cooked as purchased; larger ones with the head, tail, and fins removed are split into serving-size pieces.

Dressed fish are scaled and eviscerated at the market. The head, tail, and fins are usually removed as well. Small dressed fish are cooked as they are or split along the back and halved. Larger ones may also be cooked as they are or cut into serving-size pieces.

Steaks are the crosscut sections of larger dressed fish. They are usually one inch or more thick, and are ready to cook as purchased. Some of the largest steaks may be divided into serving-size pieces before being cooked. A small piece of backbone is usually the only bone that remains in fish steaks.

Fillets are the sides of fish cut lengthwise away from the backbone. They are usually skinned and practically boneless, thereby requiring no further preparation before cooking. A single fillet is cut from only one side of the fish. Butterfly fillets are double fillets, one from each side of the fish, held together by skin and uncut meat.

When you buy fish in the market, you will undoubtedly choose the market form to suit your individual needs. You may never need to know how to clean and dress a fish unless you are fortunate enough to have a sport fisherman share his catch with you. And even then there are few complexities to be encountered if you follow the simple instructions given below. Since virtually all fish are cleaned and dressed alike, the illustration below provided with directions, applies to most varieties of fresh- and salt-water fish.

SCALING AND CLEANING

Soak the fish in cold water before scaling, then lay it on a flat surface. Hold the fish securely by the tail with one hand. With the other hand, scrape off the scales with a knife working from tail to head. Be especially careful to

CLEAN AND DRESS SEAFOOD

remove all the scales near the base of the fins and the head. Now slit the fish's belly from the anal or ventral fin to the head. Remove the entrails.

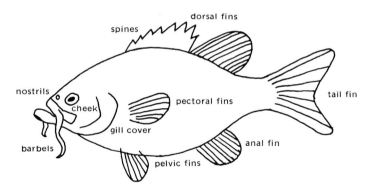

DRESSING

Cut around the anal and pelvic fins and work them free. Remove the head, including the pectoral fins, by cutting along the gill openings. You will have to cut through the backbone in order to remove these portions. The backbone is large, cut down to it on each side of the fish's head, then snap the bone by bending it over the edge of the working surface. Cut off the tail. Dislodge the dorsal or large back fin by cutting the fish along both sides of this fin. Pull the fin forward quickly toward the front of the fish, removing the fin with its root bones intact. Wash the fish in cold running water in order to rinse out any remaining membranes. The fish is now dressed and ready to be cooked.

You may cook the whole dressed fish exactly as it has been prepared or you may cut it into steaks or fillets. *To cut steaks*: cut a large dressed fish crosswise into sections about one inch thick. *To cut fillets*: With a sharp knife, slit the dressed fish along the back from the tail to the head. Then cut down to the backbone just above the collarbone. Turn the knife flat and cut the flesh lengthwise along the backbone. Cut the flesh away from the rib bones, and lift the entire side of the fish in one piece. Repeat the operation on the other side, if desired. *To skin fillets*: lay them flat on a working surface, skin side down. Holding the tail end with your fingers, cut through the flesh to the skin about one half inch from the end of the fillets. Flatten the knife on the skin and cut the flesh away from the skin by pushing the knife forward while holding the free end of the skin firmly between the fingers.

When you are ready to cook the cleaned and dressed fish, refer to the *Fish Cooking Guide* below to accurately determine the length of time required to cook many forms of fresh and frozen fish. The easy-to-read chart is divided among the seven most common methods of fish cookery. It also briefly details the recommended cooking temperatures and approximate cooking times for the most popular market forms of fish. This chart will become your handy reference guide for all fish cookery.

FISH COOKING GUIDE

COOKING METHOD	MARKET FORM	RECOMMENDED TEMPERATURE (in degrees)	APPROXIMATE TIME
Baking	Whole	400	20-25 minutes
	Fillets	400	15-20 minutes
	Frozen fried	425	15-20 minutes
Broiling	Whole		10-16 minutes (turning once)
	Fillets, steaks		10-15 minutes
	Frozen fried		10-15 minutes
Charcoal grilling	Whole	Moderate	12-18 minutes (turning once)
	Fillets, steaks	Moderate	10-12 minutes (turning once)
Deep-fat frying	Whole	350	3-5 minutes
	Fillets, steaks	350	3-5 minutes
	Frozen breaded	350	3-5 minutes
Pan-frying	Whole	Moderate	12-15 minutes (turning once)
	Fillets, steaks	Moderate	8-10 minutes (turning once)
	Frozen breaded	Moderate	8-10 minutes (turning once)
Poaching	Fillets or Steaks	Simmer	5-10 minutes
Steaming	Fillets or steaks	Boil	5-10 minutes

PHOTOGRAPHY CREDITS: Rice Council; National Fisheries Institute; U. S. Department of Commerce: National Marine Fisheries Service; Spanish Green Olive Commission; South African Rock Lobster Service Corporation; Standard Brands Products: Planter's Oil; Accent International; McIlhenny Company; Cling Peach Advisory Board; Olive Administrative Committee; Pineapple Growers Association; International Shrimp Council; Best Foods, a Division of CPC International Inc.; Apple Pantry: Washington State Apple Commission; Anderson, Clayton and Company: Seven Seas Dressing; United Fresh Fruit and Vegetable Association; Tuna Research Foundation; National Pecan Shellers and Processors Association; Pet, Inc.; National Dairy Council; California Avocado Advisory Board; Canned Salmon Institute; U. S. Trout Farmers Association; Angostura-Wuppermann Corporation; Keith Thomas Company; National Macaroni Institute; Ocean Spray Cranberries, Inc.; National Peanut Council.

Printed in the United States of America.